A PHOTOGRAPHER'S JOURN

MARCO POLO

MICHAEL YAMASHITA

Text and Photographs
by MICHAEL YAMASHITA

Historical Introductions
by GIANNI GUADALUPI

Project Manager and Editorial Director
VALERIA MANFERTO DE FABIANIS

Graphic Design
CLARA ZANOTTI

Cover Design
BILL MARR

Editorial Coordination
MARIA VALERIA URBANI GRECCHI
ENRICO LAVAGNO

English Editor
ELIZABETH BIBB

Translation Editor
PETER SKINNER

WHITE STAR
PUBLISHERS

Via Candido Sassone, 22/24
13100 Vercelli - Italia
www.whitestar.it

ISBN 88-544-005-X

REPRINT
2 3 4 5 6 07 06 05 04
Printed in Italy by
Grafiche Industriali srl, Foligno (PG)
Color separation by Fotomec, Turin

CONTENTS

PREFACE
by MICHAEL YAMASHITA   PAGE 6

HISTORICAL INTRODUCTION
Travels and adventures of Messer Milione
by GIANNI GUADALUPI   PAGE 16

PART I: FROM VENICE TO CHINA

HISTORICAL INTRODUCTION   PAGE 40
VENICE   PAGE 54
IRAQ   PAGE 72
IRAN   PAGE 116
AFGHANISTAN   PAGE 152

PART II: MARCO POLO IN CHINA

HISTORICAL INTRODUCTION   PAGE 206
FROM PAMIR TO KASHGAR   PAGE 218
FROM KASHGAR TO XANADU   PAGE 254
FROM BEJING TO JIANGSU PAGE 286
SICHUAN, YUNNAN, LAOS AND MYANMAR   PAGE 312
LABRANG AND THE TIBETAN PLATEAU   PAGE 356

PART III: THE RETURN JOURNEY

HISTORICAL INTRODUCTION   PAGE 400
QUANZHOU, THE SOUTH CHINA SEA AND VIETNAM   PAGE
INDONESIA AND SRI LANKA   PAGE 436
INDIA   PAGE 454

EPILOGUE   PAGE 496

MICHAEL YAMASHITA

a photographer's journey

PREFACE

IT ALL BEGAN WITH THE QUESTION: DID MARCO POLO GO TO CHINA?

Frances Wood, head of the Chinese Department at the British Museum, declared that he didn't, in her 1996 book of the same name. She cast doubt on Polo's credibility, her argument being largely based not on what Polo wrote about in his epic thirteenth-century travelogue, but what he left out. Wood questioned why he had not included such notable Chinese accomplishments and customs as book printing, bound feet, calligraphy, cormorant fishing, tea-drinking, chopsticks and the Great Wall.

As a professional traveler who specializes in Marco Polo territory, I felt an urge to defend this peripatetic Italian whose path I had often crossed in my work in the Far East. I have stayed in the Marco Polo Hotel in Singapore, eaten in his namesake restaurant in Venice, taken a cruise ship named for him in Hong Kong, puffed on Marco Polo cigarettes in Indonesia and shopped for clothes at the Marco Polo shop in Beijing. Could a book so widely read, a man whose name has inspired hundreds of business ventures and is on the tongue of every kid playing one of the most popular swimming pool games in America, really be a phony?

What if we were to mount an expedition to retrace the great explorer's route using his modestly titled "A Description of the World," as our guide-

book, thereby putting to rest the question once and for all? We would revisit every place Marco described and photograph evidence of what remained, albeit 700 years after he had written about it.

In researching my proposal, I found that, Frances Wood notwithstanding, Marco has a fair share of highly respectable and noted defenders. They are quick to point out that he lived among the Mongols, under the employ of Kublai Khan himself, and therefore would not have had much to do with the Chinese or their customs. He was more likely to have eaten with his hands and sipped mares' milk than to have used chopsticks or drunk tea. They point out that he alludes to book printing and bound feet in his descriptions of paper money and the distinctive gait of Chinese women. And, as for neglecting to mention the Great Wall, the fact is that it was not very great in Marco's day. The immense fortifications around Beijing we know most familiarly as the Wall were not built until three hundred years after Marco left China.

I fired off a query to Bill Allen, the editor at the National Geographic magazine where I have been working as a freelance photographer for the past 20 years. The last story done by the Geographic on Marco, titled "The World's Greatest Overland Explorer," was published in 1928. Allen was

For my mother, Kiyoko Yamashita, my greatest fan, with love

MICHAEL YAMASHITA

1 Marco Polo portrayed in an eighteenth-century watercolor.

2-3 Opium smokers in Qualeh Panjah, Afghanistan.

5 A woman in Minab, Iran in her traditional hejab.

intrigued by the idea and gave the green light. Armed with four cameras, a dozen lenses, a thousand rolls of film and a copy of his book, I set out in search of Marco Polo, often in the company of Geographic staff writer Mike Edwards, who had jumped at the chance to write the story of our journey.

But what started as a typical four-month National Geographic assignment soon became an obsession. "Marco Polo Fever " is what renowned China scholar Jonathan Spence calls it. "It is a strange disease. It can strike at any moment. The symptoms are quite clear: an overwhelming fascination with everything Marco Polo said or wrote about. There is no known cure." I have a bad case of it.

For the better part of four years now, I have been living with Marco as a close friend. He has been my most reliable guide and traveling companion, taking me thousands of miles from his birthplace in Venice (or Korcula — the Croatians claim he was born there), through the mountains and deserts of Iraq and Iran, to the war zone of Afghanistan and over the Pamir Mountains, "the roof of the world," as Marco called them, and then on through China itself.

Marco trekked along the southern Silk Road with its oasis towns of Kashgar and Hotan, over the sea of sand that is the Taklimakan desert to the Buddhist art treasures of Dunhuang and on to Inner Mongolia and Shangdu (Kublai Khan's fabled Xanadu in the Coleridge poem). He travelled into Tibet and Myanmar on business for Kublai Khan. He stayed in Yangzhou and Hangzhou (dubbed the Venice of the East), the greatest cities of the world in his day, and sailed down the Grand Canal and the Yangtze River — and so did we.

Having followed Marco's footsteps for over two years, we decided we could not leave him in China; we had to see him home by way of tropical Sumatra, Sri Lanka and coastal India. Our journey back to Italy was considerably shorter than Marco's, though; it took him 24 years to complete his roundtrip tour, three years for the return trip alone.

But unlike Marco, we had no golden tablet, or paiza, from Kublai Khan allowing us safe and unrestricted travel through all the lands in his domain, which included pretty much everything between China and what is now Eastern Europe. To travel the same route today requires much more than hopping on a horse or camel and heading toward the rising sun. Our itinerary was a logistical nightmare.

To get to Iraq, through the no-fly zone imposed by the United Nations, we flew to Jordan, then went overland by Chevy Suburban to Baghdad, where we were met by guides from the Iraqi Ministry of Foreign Affairs. Their primary job was to monitor what we saw and where we went. I was often told by our "guides" that I could not take a picture in a certain direction as there was a palace or military installation in the area and never was I allowed to shoot from a high building. In one instance, I asked my minder Mohammed if I could climb to the top of a minaret in the city of Mosul, which Marco mentioned as the source of the much coveted Mosulin (or muslin) cloth. He agreed and followed me as we climbed the narrow stairway in the dark. I bounded ahead of him, unaware that he suffered from claustrophobia and was having great difficulty keeping up with me. I got to the top and shot pictures quickly in every direction. By the time he caught up with me to give the usual "no pictures" rule, I had finished and was heading back down with a grin on my face. To get into Afghanistan, we first needed visas to Almaty, Kazakhstan, where we picked up a flight to Dushanbe, capital of Tajikistan. There we were met by soldiers from the Northern Alliance, who got us aboard one of Ahmad Shah Massoud's helicopters and flew us, hovering just above the tree line to avoid Taliban radar, to his headquarters in the Panjshir Valley. We then traveled by battered Toyota pick-up truck with our own "paiza," a letter from Massoud instructing his northern commanders to provide help, usually in the form of a Kalashnikov-armed escort, bread and kebabs and a spot on the floor for our sleeping bags.

Where Marco worried about bandits and illness (he is said to have spent a year here recuperating from malaria), we worried about land mines and car breakdowns. There are only a few vehicles available for hire in northern Afghanistan, as most have been commandeered by the warlords. Donkey cart and horse are the main forms of transportation in that sad country, much the same as in Marco's day. Thanks to our letter from Massoud, we were able to find an old Toyota pick-up to take us to the Wakhan corridor and the border of China.

Traveling over bomb-cratered roads we stopped innumerable times to fill our overheated radiator in the thin air of the Hindu Kush. At one point we even lost our steering when the rod connected to the wheels snapped. Agha, our driver, first repaired it by lashing the pieces together with yak-hair rope and driving backwards over the dry riverbed that passed for a road. That repair job lasted for less than ten minutes before we had to stop and retie it. We eventually replaced yak hair with twentieth-century Cordura nylon straps from my camera bags, but without much better results. We eventually limped into the town of Eshkashem, having covered only 30 miles in three days, about the same as Marco might have done traveling by donkey caravan. At least Marco could have eaten his broken down animal; we had no other recourse than to abandon our transport.

China, usually the toughest country for journalists to obtain travel and photography permissions, turned out to be the easiest, at least for part of our journey. The Chinese love Marco Polo. It has always been in their interest to prove Marco was for real. He was China's greatest propagandist, describing a world that, in his time, was far superior to any part in the West.

Throughout the trip, we were constantly amazed at how accurate a reporter Marco was. In Iran, he led us right to the same green hotspring he had written about. In Hormuz on the Persian Gulf, we encountered the "black-skinned Muslims," descendants of African slaves, that he mentioned. In Afghanistan, we found his "mountains of salt" outside Taloqan and the bighorn sheep named for him (*Ovis poli*, or Marco Polo sheep) in the Wakhan corridor. In China, we saw the jade mines of Hotan, the singing sand dunes of Dunhuang and the huge reclining Buddha in Zhangye, all documented by Marco. We met the "people with gold teeth," and "raw meat eaters" at Erhai Lake. With each triumphant find, I became more and more convinced that Marco had to have been writing from first-hand experience. Not only were these sights exactly as he described, but we found each precisely where he told us to look.

Every day, more and more passages of his book came to life. Even his descriptions of the people he met along the way held true. He tells of the Afghans — "a warlike race who worship Mohammed ... they speak a language of their own and are valiant soldiers." Marco could have been describing the commander Massoud, who defeated the Russians and held the Taliban at bay until he was assassinated a few days before September 11, 2001. The Tibetan monks Marco described as having "huge monasteries of such a size that some resemble small cities inhabited by more than 2000 monks" and who "wear their heads and chins clean-shaven and lead a life of great austerity, and all their lives long they eat nothing but bran" could have been the monks I met at Labrang Monastery, in Gansu, who today still eat their tsampa, barleymeal mixed with yak-butter tea.

By the end of our journey, I was a true believer, feeling linked to Marco as a kindred spirit. On a beach in Kerala, India, I felt Marco's presence as I witnessed a scene that seemed straight out of the thirteenth century —hundreds of half-naked fisherman rhythmically pulling in their nets, with nothing of the current century as far as my long-lensed eye could see. No motors, just oars; no Nikes or printed t-shirts, just bare feet and loin cloths. I imagined Marco watching fishermen like these in awe, as I did, shooting roll after roll trying to capture it all in one frame. I contemplated that if Marco were alive today, he surely would have been one of us, a writer or photographer for the National Geographic.

The climax to my travels with Marco came a few weeks later when I stopped by the Columbus Library in Seville, Spain to photograph Christopher Columbus's well-worn copy of Marco's book, complete with his own five-hundred year old doodles. I thumbed through the pages looking for the best of his jottings that I could find in the margins, suppressing an urge to lick my fingers to turn the pages of the 15th-century volume. I chose a page describing a scene in India along the very coast where I had photographed the fishermen and their nets. Columbus had highlighted a

11 Traveling on the Pamir Plateau, China and on the Khunjerab Pass (border between China and Pakistan).

12-13 Tajik children of an elementary school in Taxkorgan, Xinjiang, China.

14-15 Tibetan monks in Labrang, Gansu, China.

passage by sketching a pointed hand. Then it hit me. Christopher Columbus, like me, must have had a bad case of Polo fever, dreaming about the lands as described by Marco, making note of the places he hoped to discover.

And just as now there are naysayers, there were doubtless an equal share of them in Marco's, as well as Columbus's, time. But my by-now old friend Marco had inspired a far greater number of devotees, a list of explorers going back 700 years, from the likes of Columbus dreaming of new worlds to find, to me finding old worlds to rediscover, worlds that Messer Polo described with such accuracy and wonder. I feel proud to have gotten to know him so well.

On his deathbed, Marco is reported to have said "I have not told half of what I have seen." Marco, I wish you were alive today, to tell us more, as I would gladly follow you on another adventure.

The result of our long journey in the footsteps of Marco Polo culminated in an unprecedented three-part series that ran in the summer of 2001 in the National Geographic, that appeared with text authored by my colleague and frequent traveling companion, Mike Edwards. The last time the Geographic had covered Marco was in 1928, when they proclaimed him to be "the world's greatest overland traveler". And after following him for over two years, there's no doubt he retains that title.

GIANNI GUADALUPI

TRAVELS *AND* ADVENTURES

of Messer
MILIONE

I N SUMMER 1298 THE WINDS OF WAR WERE BLOWING IN THE ADRIATIC.

The Genoese fleet – eighty five galleys which, for the first time, had three men per oar and many highly skilled bowmen on board – was under the command of Lamba Doria who ran it up and down the maze of islands on Venice's Dalmatian coastline, raiding and laying waste at will. Thus provoked, La Serenissima hurriedly armed an equally powerful squadron of ninety eight ships and placed it under the command of Andrea Dandolo, a sailor as great as his rival. But owing to the haste in which they were picked, the crews were inexperienced, mostly Lombards who had never seen the sea.

For several days the Genoese admiral dodged engagement until he was forced into the area of water between the islands of Korcula, Meleda and Lagosta where his smaller number of ships turned out to be an advantage. Doria decided to accept the challenge on 8 September, the day of the Birth of the Madonna, who was the patron saint of Genoa; in those more pious days, divine intervention was always beseeched. The night before the battle, he detached fifteen ships from his fleet with the order that they should hide behind Lagosta until battle had begun and then attack the enemy from the rear.

When the sun arose, the two formations maneuvered under the power of oars and attacked one another with ferocity. Arrows and incendiary missiles flew. Luck first seemed to favor the Venetians; the son of Lamba Doria was killed by an arrow and his father, like an ancient Roman, ordered his body to be thrown into the sea so it did not encumber the main deck of the flagship. But when the fifteen Genoese ships appeared by surprise behind the Venetian semicircle, those who already believed themselves to be the winners fell into disorder, lost heart and were gripped by panic. Eighty four galleys out of ninety eight fell into the hands of the Genoese and over seven thousand prisoners were taken, including Andrea Dandolo, who, it is said, killed himself soon after by banging his head against the rowing bench to which he was chained. After returning to Genoa in triumph, Lamba Doria was rewarded with a palace and perpetual exemption from taxes, and the Madonna was given a gilded cloak, a gift that is renewed every 8 September.

One of the seven thousand unfortunate prisoners taken to the Ligurian capital was the captain of a galley named Marco Polo. With his compatriots, he was sent to the Malapaga prisons close to the port, or perhaps in some warehouse or store requisitioned for the purpose because Genoa was already brimful with prisoners – from another war. Thousands of Pisans had been captured in 1284 at the naval battle of Meloria when Genoa had definitively crushed its rival Pisa. Those Pisans who had not already died of hardship or disease or who had not already been ransomed, languished in the city. Among these many military men, there was one who preferred to wield a pen: his name was Rustichello or Rusticiano. Before ending in a Genoese prison, he earned a living by writing or rewriting knightly romances that were then the most common form of popular literature; they provided amusement for ladies and knights – not peasants and

19 left The galley commanded by Marco Polo prepares to enter the action at Korcula.

19 right Portrait of Marco Polo kept in the Conference Hall of Palazzo Doria Tursi in Genoa.

plebs as commoners were referred to in those days. During this period each form of literature had its own language: religious and scientific works were written in Latin, love songs in Oc (Provençal), and the astounding exploits of the Orlandos and Rinaldos were recounted in Oïl (the forerunner of modern French). Although he was Italian, Rustichello wrote in the Oïl language, just like all his fellow Italian authors of what Dante called romantic prose works.

On one of the long, tedious days of captivity, the two prisoners – the newly arrived Marco Polo and the veteran Rustichello (he had already been there for fourteen years) – met and made friends. Apart from the shortage of food and the overcrowding, the condi-

tions of the inmates were not particularly hard. They enjoyed a certain freedom of movement even if they were unable to leave their assigned enclosure, and they were able to pass the time as they chose, to receive visits, and to purchase better food, clothes or anything else that they needed. In this case, what were required were paper, a pen and ink as the Venetian had begun to the tell the Pisan, who was avid for news of the outside world, of the journeys he had made during his youth to unheard of countries, or rather of his single, incredible journey to the other end of the earth where Mongols reigned over the immense expanse of Asia that never ended, and of their leader, the Great Khan, whose high functionary Marco had become.

To Rustichello, these seemed like the stories he used to read and write, though better because they were narrated by an eye-witness and were set in exotic settings, an Elsewhere of which nobody in Europe knew anything. Cathay was a country that, in the geography of a writer of romances, bordered on the Camelot of King Arthur and on the Gog and Magog where Alexander the Great had shut up the giants. Rustichello recognized in Marco Polo's personal exploits the best imaginable plot for a book that would bring fame and fortune to both of them. It was of course a book to write in Oïl, the language of the courts. Thus Marco began to tell his story carefully and his enchanted listener to write. It also seems that there was more than one enchanted listener, and not only fellow prisoners, but Genoese 'noble gentlemen' that queued in the prison to see and 'spoil' Marco and to bring him gifts. At a certain point 'the whole city was present.' Perhaps this version was a little too panegyrical and should be treated with a pinch of salt: it was written by Giovanni Battista Ramusio, a Venetian curator of a large collection of travel writings who wrote almost three centuries later. Nonetheless, it is very probable that during his period in Genoa Marco Polo met Genoese merchants that he had come to know during his wanderings in Asia; there were many of them to be found along the route from the Black Sea to Cathay, and in Cathay itself as has been shown in modern times by the discovery of various forms of documentation, for example, tomb inscriptions. Certainly, the Venetian was not the only European, nor even the only Italian, to visit the Far East during the thirteenth century, but he was the only one to write about or dictate his experiences for the broad public.

After a few months, a book was written with Rustichello's help and published with the title *Le Devisement du Monde* (The Description of the World), also referred to as the *Livre des Merveilles* (Book of Marvels) due to the amazing tales it told; to us it is known by the concise and graphic title *Il Milione* (The Million). However, in certain codices the title *Romance of the Great Khan* is given, which suggests that many, maybe most, of its readers saw it as a work of fiction rather than as a travel book. Yet it met with immediate success and sold widely for the period. The surviving 150 or so manuscripts in libraries and archives in Europe were written in various languages: Latin, Tuscan, Venetian, French-Italian, French, etc. No two are alike and studying this host of versions is like wandering through a maze. Philologists still debate which is the closest to the missing original. For example, a codex in the Biblioteca Riccardiana in Florence is the Italian translation of the Latin text, but the Latin version was the translation of a Tuscan text, which was the translation of a Venetian copy, which was the translation of a French version, but not even that was the original in the Oïl language written by Rustichello in prison. The variances between the copies are however minor and the substance of Marco Polo's account remains unaltered.

It also seems that an early, succinct version of *Il Milione* existed written by Polo himself before he finished up a prisoner in Genoa and met his ghost-writer. It was common in Venice and all the trading cities in the Italian peninsula for merchants returning from trips to little or even unknown regions to compile an account of their trip with a summary of the goods produced there, the prices, duties, customs procedures, and the economic advantages and disadvantages of the place; in addition there

Farewell
to Constantinople

"For let me tell you that since our Lord God did mould with his hands our First Father Adam, even until this day, never hath there been Christian, or Pagan, or Tartar, or Indian, or man of any nation, who in his own person hath had so much knowledge and experience of the divers parts of the World and its Wonders as hath has Messer Marco!"

The Travels of Marco Polo, *Prologue.*

22 The Polo brothers prepare to set off: on the left, a salute to the Emperor; on the right, farewell to the Pope.

might be a section of observations on its politics, society and customs. Various examples of these 'trading manuals,' written to facilitate future journeys, exist written by Florentines, Genoese and others. It is probable that Marco Polo had begun to put down on paper what he remembered from the innumerable things he had seen at the invitation of the authorities. An inventory compiled in 1351 of the items belonging to the Doge of Venice, Marin Faliero, cites a book 'written by the hand of Marco Polo' entitled *De Locis Mirabilibus Tartarorum* (The Wondrous Regions of the Tartars). This presumed autograph text was probably the kernel around which Rustichello embroidered his literary work *Il Milione*. Ramusio says that when the two sat down to work, Marco had 'his writings and written records' sent from Venice. Ramusio also gave his explanation for the imperious title of the book: Messer Milion (M. Million) was a nickname

given to Marco Polo by his Venetian listeners who gathered in his house to hear straight from the horse's mouth of the extent of the marvels in Asia. This hyperbolic figure occurred over and over in all his tales: the Mongol armies comprised millions of horsemen, millions of junks plowed the seas and rivers of Cathay, the land itself had millions of cities, which paid millions in tributes, and so on. It seems that these numbers were considered a massive overstatement to Europeans, who were accustomed to dealing in much more modest figures, and that this reflected poorly on the credibility of the narrator: his 'Devisement du Monde' too often tipped over into the 'Romance of the Great Khan'. But whereas the book was read in the castles of Europe as though it were the most recent and exotic chapter in the adventures of the Round Table, the learned men of science and letters were much less skeptical. The doctor and philosopher Pietro d'Abano (1257-1315)

23 Nicolò and Maffeo set sail towards the venetian port of Soldaia, in Crimea.

called Marco Polo not a storyteller but 'the greatest traveler of all time, a diligent investigator of the world.' Soon the reports on the Far East contained in the book (backed up by other accounts of that far-off land, merchants' reports, and letters which are occasionally traced today in the dust of the most diligently searched archives) passed into the work of mapmakers, and Cathay and Cipango (Japan) appeared as if from nowhere. It was in search of Cipango, which Marco described as overflowing with gold, that Christopher Columbus set off in 1492 and he remained convinced until his death that even if he did not actually find it, as the gold was much less abundant than expected, he had come very close.

On the author of the book and his family we know very little more than *Il Milione* tells us, despite it also being an autobiography. The story begins shortly before Marco's birth in 1254 when two brothers, the merchants Nicolò and Maffeo Polo, set out for the Lev-

ant from Venice, the former leaving his wife pregnant. Some time later we find them in Constantinople, where Venetians felt quite at home as they had defeated the Byzantine empire in 1204 with the help of the Frankish knights in the Fourth Crusade and split the booty between them. Another consequence was that the Doge of Venice became the 'lord of a quarter and a half of the Roman empire' as his new title proudly declared. The two Polos concluded excellent business there and found themselves with a fine nest-egg which they hoped to increase further. They invested their earnings in precious stones, which formed a load that required very little space and could be easily hidden, for example, by sewing them into their clothes, and then went to offer them to clients who would certainly appreciate them: the Mongol chiefs who had conquered the steppes around the Volga in the reign of Genghis Khan and governed them ever since. Wearing shabby clothing so as not to arouse attention, and carrying little baggage but a large number of gems, they boarded a ship that took them to the Crimea. The southern coast of this region was ruled by the Venetians' rivals, the Genoese, and filled with Italians who traded with the Tartars. The brothers purchased horses and set off through the marshes and forests, meadows and salt-flats north-east toward the city of Bulgar, a huge agglomeration of wooden houses and tents overlooking the Volga and where Berke Khan resided.

Berke welcomed them with great hospitality and the Venetians, familiar with Mongol customs, 'gave' them all those jewels. Their gift was returned in money worth a sum double that which they had paid to purchase it. Mongol etiquette was such that great lords never 'bought' but received gifts which they repaid generously. The Polos were very satisfied with their profits and thought that the moment had arrived to return home, but fate lengthened their journey enormously and led them to the eastern tip of Asia. The peace that had reigned across the immense continent for decades was unexpectedly broken by the death of the Great Khan, Mongke, and by the war of succession between the claimants to the throne. Berke, who was one, went to war against his rival Argun and this turn of events made the journey back to the Crimea impossible. There was a safer, but much longer, alternative, the caravan route that wound around the Caspian Sea to Persia, which was also in the hands of a Mongol dynasty, the Hulagu. And so in 1264 Nicolò and Maffeo entered what remained of Bukhara, once a flourishing Moslem city in central Asia that had been destroyed by Genghis Khan forty years earlier, and which,

though it was still an important trading center, had never recovered from its disaster. It was here that the Polos had an encounter that was to change their lives completely.

An ambassador of Hulagu Khan had come to the city on his way to the court of Hulagu's brother, Kublai Khan, the ruler of an endless and remote region in eastern Asia called Cathay. The ambassador was surprised to find two 'Latins' in Bukhara where Europeans had not set foot for a very long time. He invited them to accompany him because he knew that Kublai would be very pleased if he arrived with Europeans in tow. It did not take much to convince the Venetians, who were excited at the prospect of being the first Westerners to enter a still virgin market. After crossing all of Asia from west to east, the two brothers finally presented themselves to Kublai Khan, who received them 'with great cheer and welcome.' After he had quizzed them on Christianity, the Pope and the Emperor, he charged them with a mission of his own. They were to travel to the Vatican in the company of his Mongol 'baron' and ask the Pope to send one hundred learned men to Cathay to preach the Christian faith to his citizens, and also to send as a gift a bottle of the oil that burned in the lamp in the Holy Sepulcher in Jerusalem.

So Maffeo and Nicolò set out happily on their return bearing a letter of safe conduct from the Great Khan written on a 'tablet of gold'; they arrived alone in the Mediterranean port of Laiazzo in the kingdom of Little Armenia because the Mongol 'baron' had fallen sick on the journey and remained behind.

It was January or February 1269 and the pope to whom they were to convey their letter from Kublai Khan, Clement IV, had died in November. Moreover, it was to be three years

24 The Polos arrive in Bukhara where they met the Great Khan's ambassador, who invited them to meet the Khan.

25 top Kublai, the 'Lord of all the Tartars in the world', welcomes the brothers before his imperial tent.

25 bottom Nicolò and Maffeo present the Khan with gifts sent by the Pope: a gold cross and an exquisite codex.

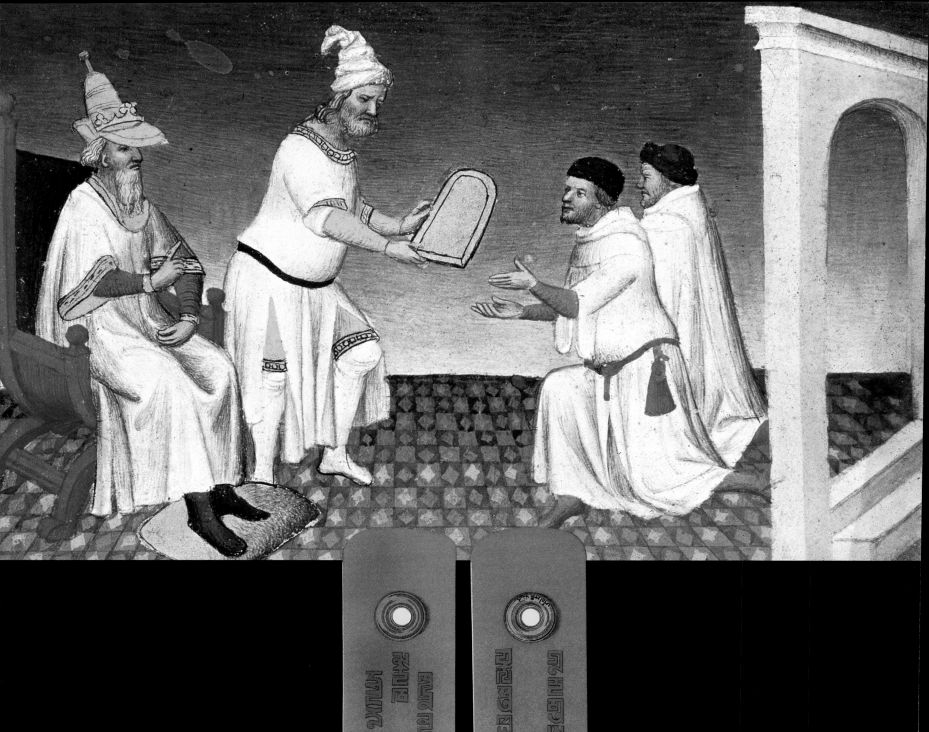

26 top Kublai hands them the paiza (safe-conduct) engraved on a gold tablet.

26 bottom Two original paiza, found in Siberia.

27 Marco Polo enters the scene: departure from Jerusalem with his father and uncle in 1271.

before a new pope was elected and the Polo brothers, who were waiting for the conclave to elect Clement's successor, decided to return to Venice to see their families.

On their arrival, Nicolò learnt that his wife had died fourteen years earlier giving birth to their son, Marco, who had never seen his father. It is easy to imagine with what excitement the young Marco listened to the stories his father and uncle told of their adventurous journey.

The Polos remained in Venice until spring 1271 in the expectation that a pope would be elected but then they lost patience and started out once more for the Levant, this time taking Marco with them. They disembarked at Acre in Palestine, which was the last outpost of the Crusader kingdom of Jerusalem and where they met the papal legate, Tedaldo Visconti of Piacen-

za, whom they told of the mission they had been charged with by the Great Khan and the impossibility of discharging it without a pope. With the authorization of Tedaldo, they went to the Holy Sepulcher in Jerusalem where they took some of the oil and then moved on to Laiazzo in Armenia to organize their journey back to Cathay. This was where they met with their first surprise: the assembly of cardinals in Viterbo had finally elected a new pope; it was Tedaldo Visconti himself, who took the name of Gregory X. Tedaldo heard the news while he was still in Acre and called the Polos back to the city where he gave them messages for Kublai Khan before departing for Rome to be crowned pope. As for the one hundred learned men, he only had a couple to hand, the Dominicans Nicolò da Vincenza and Guglielmo da Tripoli, who left with the Polos for Laiazzo but who soon lost heart and returned.

28 The dangers of travel: a 'wild man' and a lion lie in wait for two travelers.

In the meantime, war had broken out between the Sultan of Egypt and the King of Little Armenia and the risk existed of the Venetians falling into the hands of the Egyptian cavalry, whose reputation was terrible. Yet without worrying too much, the three continued with their preparations, perhaps even glad to be free of the two friars who were unaccustomed to hardship. At the start of 1272 they were on the road to Mount Ararat where Noah's ark had run aground after the Flood receded and where Marco found a spring of oil that would burn. Then they headed towards Mosul where they had clothes spun with gold silk, and from there to Baghad and Basra where they took ship for the Persian Gulf and Hormuz, the port where ships converged bearing spices, ivory, jewels and fabrics from India. They wanted to continue from Hormuz by sea but they eventually chose to journey on by land and to cross the salt desert of Kerman to reach Badakhshan. Here they were forced to halt for an entire year because Marco had fallen sick in the torrid climate, but the young boy took advantage of the break to study languages and, when he was finally presented to Kublai Khan, he was already a polyglot like his father and uncle. The journey restarted

29 A merchant ship approaches Hormuz, from where the Polos hoped to sail for India.

and crossed the Pamir plateau where there are flocks of large horned sheep that zoologists were to name *Ovis poli*. The group descended into the jade regions of Kashgar, Yarkand and Hotan near Lake Lob, towns that would only see Europeans again in the second half of the nineteenth century. The terrible Gobi Desert did not stop them although for the thirty interminable days of its crossing they were tormented by diabolical voices that called their names, by cavalcades of specters and by evil spirits that filled the air with the sounds of trumpets, drums and gongs. When they reached Tangut, on

the edge of the Mongolian steppes, they were like the survivors of a shipwreck, but here they were met by a delegation sent by the Great Khan whose messengers had given notice of the Venetians' expected arrival.

They saw Kublai Khan once more in 1275 in his summer residence of K'aiping-fu (Xanadu) in the region of Dolon Nor. The ruler of half of Asia received them in a huge bamboo pavilion supported by gilded columns decorated with sculpted dragons. The pavilion stood in the middle of a park surrounded by a wall sixteen miles long on each side in which deer of all sorts grazed; Kublai

Kublai Khan enthusiastically receives the Venetian travelers at court with gi[...] [...]le representation of the 'gold-roofed' palace belonging to the Emperor of Cipa[...]

them, either with a hawk or a tame leopard [...] him on the saddle of his horse. Particularly [...]t Khan appreciated the gifts from the Pope [...]elicacy not to notice the absence of the one [...] men, perhaps on which he had not counted [...]en he asked who was the fearless youth that [...]them (Marco had just passed this twenty-[...]. 'This is my son', replied Nicolò, 'and your [...]lal formula with which Marco was placed at [...]n of the Emperor of Cathay. The Khan [...]co into his retinue, so beginning a relation-[...] to last for seventeen years to mutual satis-[...]Great Khan particularly appreciated two of [...]his powers of observation and the ability to [...]e had seen with the art of a born narrator

Consequently, without giving him any pa[...] he sent Marco on several missions in [...] Cathay (northern China) and to Mangi (C[...] Yellow River) where the Khan's troops [...] their occupation. Thus Marco Polo visite[...] the enormous empire; he traveled far sou[...] the borders of Tibet and modern Myann[...] news of countries that he did not see [...] Cipangu (Japan), which he heard flowed [...] also reputed to have been the governor of [...] chow for three years, and all this while his[...] toured China, enriching themselves wit[...] jewels, their specialty. Kublai also made [...] Venetians as military experts, and asked th[...] machines to take the cities that resisted M[...]

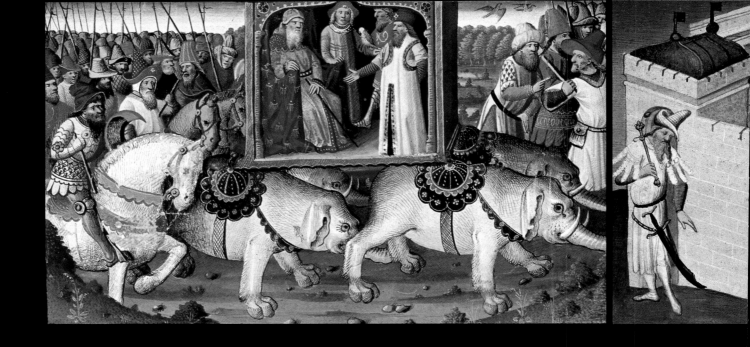

32 top left Hunting in a litter, with an escort of '10,000 hawkers'.

32-33 top center Kublai Khan's winter residence in Khanbaliq (modern Beijing).

33 top right The Khan prepares to go big-game hunting with lions and dogs.

The GREAT KHAN'S Court

32 bottom left The Great Khan dines with three
wives and some dignitaries.

32 bottom center left Four of Kublai's wives, each
accompanied by one of their children, chat.

32-33 bottom center right Elephant-hunting in
the kingdom of Myen (Myanmar).

33 bottom right Described by Marco Polo, the
gavials of Yunnan were transformed into dragons

34 A group of travelers disembark to encounter elephants, eagles and griffins.

The years passed and their imperial favor did not seem to diminish; the Great Khan was very affectionate toward the Polos — to the extent that they doubted they would ever see their homeland again. But once more fate brought a turning point in their lives. In 1286, Argun Khan, the ruler of Persia, lost his beloved wife, Bolgana, who was Kublai's great-niece. The last wish of the dying woman was that Argun send an ambassador to the emperor of Cathay to ask Kublai to send her husband another wife from her own Mongol tribe. The ambassadors arrived, and Kublai happily chose the beautiful seventeen-year-old Koekoecin, but a war had just broken out in central Asia and the delegation could not return by the same route that they had taken to Cathay.

As chance had it, Marco was just then returning from a long trip down the Chinese coast and he was able to report on the safety and ease of navigation of the route. The Persian ambassadors seized the chance and asked the Great Khan to let them return home by sea accompanied by the three Venetians. At the start of 1292, fourteen large junks set sail from the large port of Zaiton carrying the princess, the ambassadors, the three Venetians and a huge retinue.

35 The kingdom of Eli (perhaps Kerala) was also populated by various fauna, in part chimerical.

However, the journey was not as free from diffi- culty as Marco had foreseen and interminable halts had to be made in Sumatra, Ceylon and southern India. It took two years before the coast of Persia was sighted, during which time two of the three ambassa- dors had died, only eighteen of the six hundred sol- diers had survived, and of the large retinue of servants and maids of honor, only one remained. Marco did not explain the reasons for this disaster but it was proba- bly simply the result of the normal risks of a sea jour- ney in that time: monsoons, pirates, sickness, etc.

Once arrived in Persia, the survivors discovered that the intended husband, Argun, was also dead and that the crown had passed to his son, but he was still a child and ruled under a regent. The potentially embarrassing problem of the redundant betrothed was resolved by assigning the Mongol princess to the heir. But the series of deaths was not yet finished because news shortly arrived that Kublai himself had passed on to a better life at the age of eighty. The three Venetians asked the princess permission to take their leave to return home and, on their departure, she burst into tears because, after so many dramatic experiences together, she 'loved them like fathers.'

The Polos headed towards Venice via Tabriz, Trebisond and Constantinople, and eventually reached home in 1295. It is said that on their arrival home, no-one recognized them 'as happened to Ulysses who returned to Ithaca after twenty years in Troy' comments Ramusio. To convince their friends and relatives of their identity, the three laid on a lavish banquet and dressed in increasingly magnificent clothes for each course. At the end they put on the shabby loose Tartar jackets that they had worn on their arrival in Venice and took out from the linings a cascade of dazzling rubies, sapphires, carbuncles, diamonds and other precious stones. The display astonished the onlookers and convinced them more than any argument. But they had also brought home other goods, like soft yak hides and the seeds of a plant that provided pigment, perhaps indigo, which Marco had purchased in Sumatra and tried, in vain, to raise in the Venetian lagoon. And of course they had innumerable memories and astounding stories to tell that left the other merchants of the Serenissima filled with envy.

Then came the war with Genoa, the disastrous battle, the prison and the meeting with Rustichello. Freed after a year, Marco returned to Venice where he had a wife named Donata who had given him three daughters, Fantina, Bellela and Moreta, but no son who could follow in his father's footsteps to the far side of eastern Asia.

Marco died in 1324 as a highly honored citizen of Venice. It is said that his friends, seeing him on the point of death, asked him to save his soul by confessing that he had told a pack of fictitious stories in his book. To which the dying man replied indignantly that "he had not even told them the half of it."

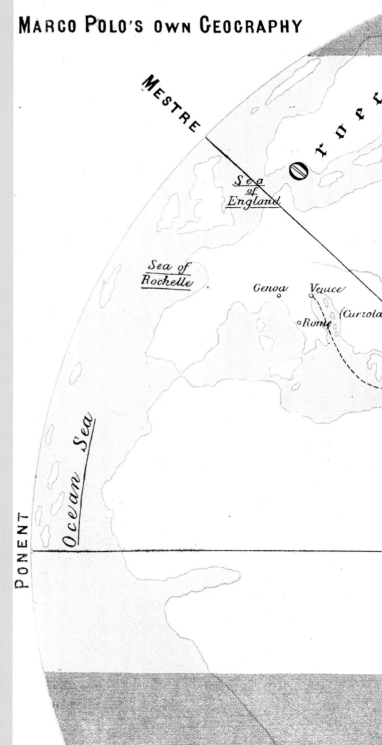

Probable View
·OF·
MARCO POLO'S OWN GEOGRAPHY

36-37 The map from the 'Travels of Marco Polo,' by Sir Henry Yule.

38-39 Satellite view of the Eurasia with Marco Polo's routes.

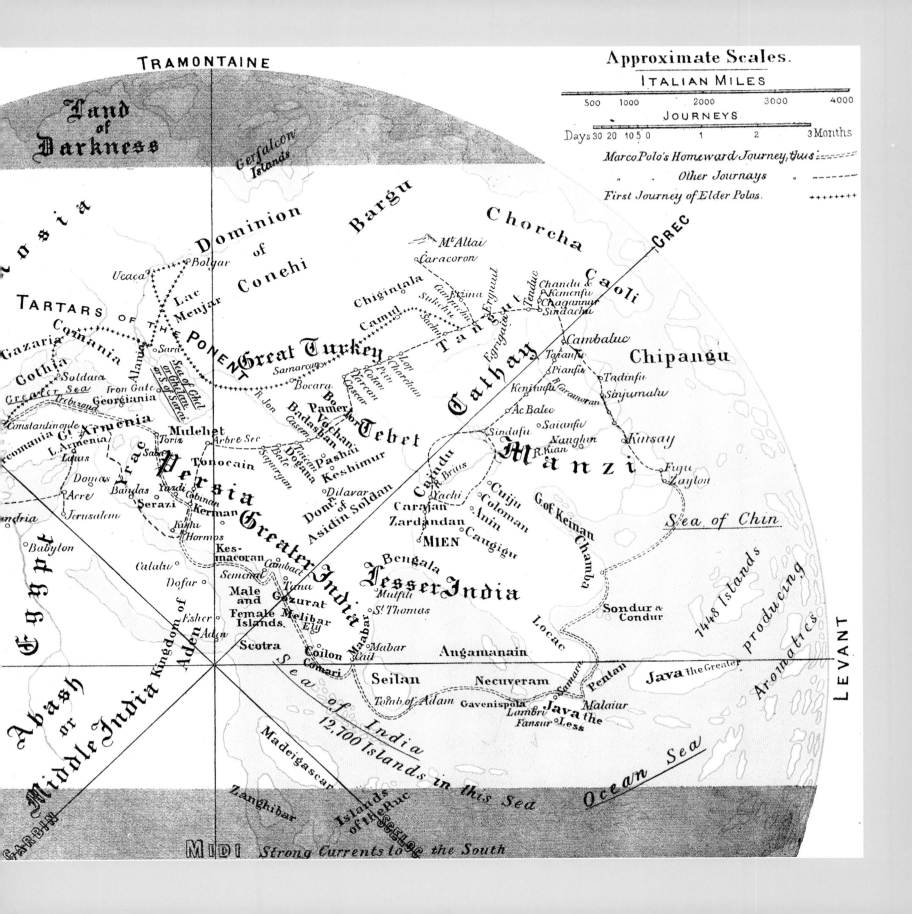

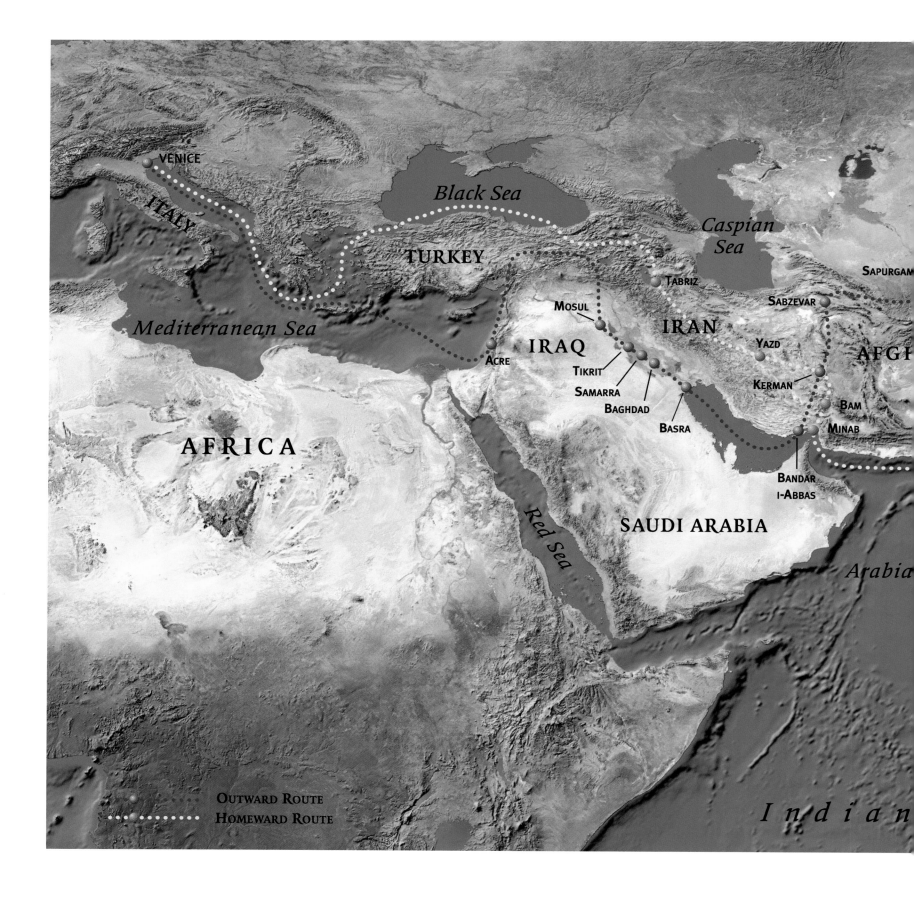

VENICE

Black Sea

Caspian Sea

ITALY

TURKEY

SAPURGAM

TABRIZ

SABZEVAR

MOSUL

IRAN

Mediterranean Sea

IRAQ

YAZD

AFGI

ACRE

TIKRIT

KERMAN

BAM

SAMARRA

BAGHDAD

MINAB

BASRA

AFRICA

SAUDI ARABIA

BANDAR
i-ABBAS

Red Sea

Arabia

OUTWARD ROUTE
HOMEWARD ROUTE

Indian

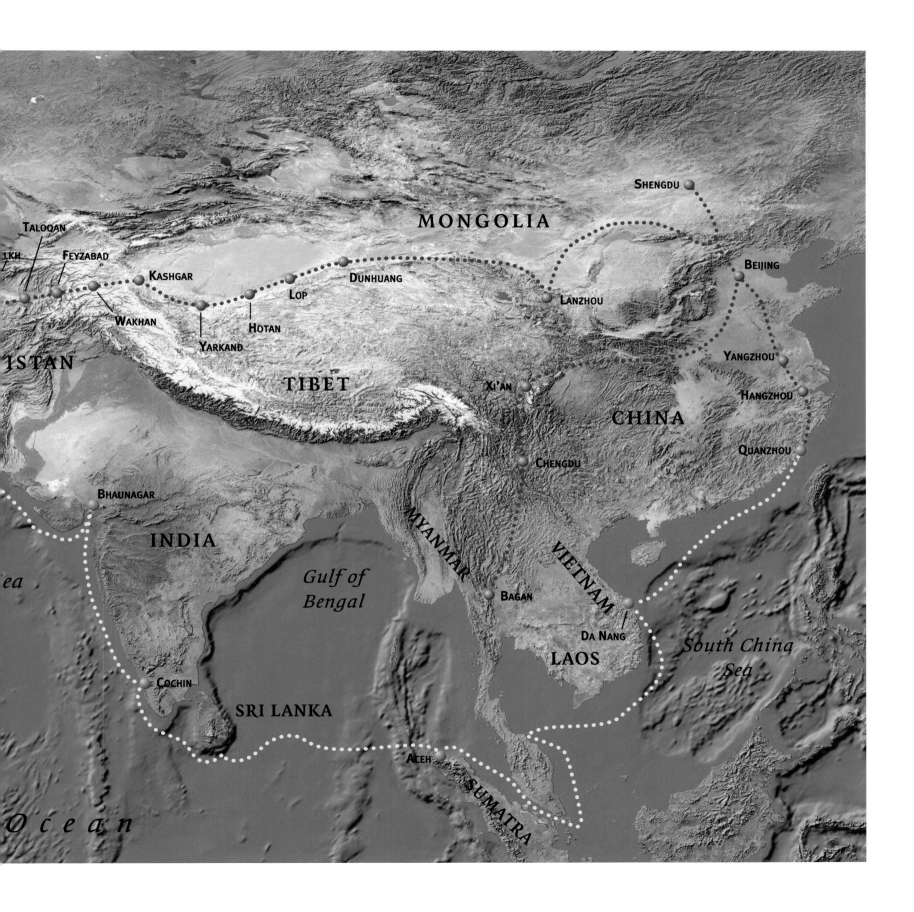

FROM VENICE to CHINA

INTRODUCTION

'PROTECT, O LORD, YOUR FAITHFUL SAILORS FROM STORMS, PROTECT THEM FROM SUDDEN SHIPWRECK AND FROM THE EVIL DOINGS OF WILY ENEMIES.'

This was the invocation used by Venetian sailors in their attempt to propitiate the treacherous sea before embarking on a voyage, and it also passed into the Venetian ceremony of the *Sposalizio del mare* (Marriage of the Sea) during which the Doge of the Serenissima threw a simple gold ring into the water each Ascension Day. The prayer was also recited by a priest when large merchant convoys, called *mude*, comprising thirty or forty vessels – galleys and sailboats of different tonnages escorted by several war-ships – set sail around Easter time and again at the beginning of autumn each year. The *muda* that set out in spring 1271 included two brothers, Nicolò and Maffio Polo, and Nicolò's son, the seventeen-year-old Marco. They left to keep their word given to the Great Khan to return to his court, even if they were unable to satisfy his wish of taking one hundred Christian preachers with them to the empire of Cathay. The reason was that the papal throne had been vacant for more than two years because the conclave of cardinals was unable to agree on a satisfactory candidate, and without a

pope there was no possibility of organizing so numerous a body of missionaries.

No matter, thought the Polos, the benevolent Kublai Khan will understand and there is no more time to be lost. The Polos had the diplomatic contacts between the two ends of the world very much at heart, but even more important to them were their own commercial interests.

The fleet of Venetian vessels slowly sailed down the eastern coast of the Adriatic, that maze of islands and peninsulas in Dalmatia over which the Republic of St. Mark ruled unchallenged. The fleet stopped every so often to take on fresh water and foodstuffs. In those times, sea voyages above all hugged the coast, with the ships slipping along the shoreline as though they were being carried by a river current, always in sight of land so that they could take refuge in the event of storms or pirates. Perhaps on one of those days, the young Marco made out the island of Curzola (Korcula) on the horizon; Curzola was the final possession before Venetian Dalmatia gave way to the stretch belonging to Ragusa, the Republic's marine rival. He may even have set foot there in one of the fleet's stops, without having an inkling that thirty or so years later these waters were to be the setting for a dramatic event in his life.

43 Marco, Nicolò and Maffeo Polo set sail from Venice for St. John d'Acre.

44 The Polos exchange a last goodbye with their relations at the gates of a 'land-based' Venice.

At the entrance to the Adriatic – which was known as the Gulf of Venice because the lagoon city was master of all of it – the large fleet split into five smaller *mude* whose destinations were different. The Puglia *muda*, which was carrying cereals from Trani to Otranto, had already practically arrived. The Romanian *muda* would slip down the Peloponnese (then known as Morea) and sail up toward Constantinople through the dozens of islands in the Aegean. The *muda* heading for Barberia was to head west through the Sicilian channel and along the North African coast to Morocco. The Egyptian convoy had Alexandria as its destination where it would purchase spices from the Asiatic archipelagoes. And the

Syrian *muda* was aiming for Acre where it would drop the pilgrims traveling to the Holy Land and the three Polos.

The heavily fortified city of Acre was just then all that remained of the Kingdom of Jerusalem founded by the Crusaders a couple of centuries earlier. It stood on a small peninsula circled by turreted walls and its port was at times so crowded that many ships were obliged to anchor out at sea. The city was divided into quarters – also walled – because they contained rival communities such as Venetians and Genoese who fought ferociously. The city was a small area of houses, churches, warehouses and narrows streets threaded by Arab merchants, European

45 Having arrived in the Holy Land, the Venetians visit the Holy Sepulcher in Jerusalem.

pilgrims and clergy, Knights Templar with their red cross, Teutonic knights with their black cross, and Knights Hospitaler with the scarlet Maltese cross on their long white cloaks.

During this period, two outstanding figures resided in Acre: Prince Edward of England with his retinue of English knights (a year later, right in the center of the city, he was stabbed with the poisoned dagger of an Assassin and escaped death by a whisker), and the papal legate Tedaldo Visconti.

After taking lodgings in the Venetian quarter of the city and being presented to the bailo (the Venetian representative in Acre), the Polos went to see Visconti. They told him of their mission and received

authorization from him to take some of the oil that burned in the lamp in the Church of the Holy Sepulcher in Jerusalem; this was so that they could fulfill one of Kublai's other requests, as the sovereign wished to present it to his Christian mother.

After traveling to Jerusalem to take the oil and returning to Acre, probably with one of the caravans of pilgrims, the three Polos took their leave of Visconti, bearing a message from the legate for the Great Khan. They embarked for the port of Laiazzo in the kingdom of Little Armenia, which was the Mediterranean terminal for caravans arriving from central Asia and Persia. This was where, in the words of Marco, 'all the spices and all the cloths of silk and gold from the interior with all the other precious goods' were taken. It was another maritime city filled with merchants of every nationality, above all the great rivals, the Venetians and Genoese.

Before being able to organize their enormously long journey along the Silk Road, the Polos received surprising news: not only had the conclave in Viterbo finally elected a new pope, they had nominated Tedaldo Visconti. He now recalled the three Venetians to Acre where he wished to see them before departing for Rome and his coronation. Gregory X – this was the name he took – blessed them, supplied them with more authoritative missives and appointed two friars to accompany them on their journey to the Great Khan, though they were a very poor substitute for the one hundred requested. Unfortunately, there were no more to hand in the Catholic Levant, which was in any case about to be reabsorbed into the empire of the Mamelukes. However, the two friars were not destined to arrive in Cathay, nor did they even begin on the journey because, once they had arrived in Laiazzo, the two lost heart after hearing of the war being fought between the Armenians and the Sultan of Babylonia (the title given by Europeans of that time to the Mameluke ruler in Cairo).

The three Venetians therefore continued alone, being either fearless or very sure of the passes of safeconduct they had received from the Khan, because the long arm of the Mongols was still feared in those parts. They passed through insalubrious Little Armenia and entered the Turkmen region governed by the Seljuks, i.e. Anatolia, that had once been part of the Byzantine empire, where the Turks that bred horses and mules spoke 'a foul language.' Armenians and Greeks lived in the cities as craftsmen and traders. Here 'the best carpets in the world and of the loveliest color' were made. Great Armenia, on the other hand, was the source of the best 'bucherame' in the world (a delicate transparent material greatly prized in the Middle Ages). In this region the Polos also saw the broad base Mount Ararat that took more than two days to skirt and on which Noah's ark was said to have come to rest, but no-one was able to climb it due to the large and permanent quantity of snow on its peak.

Then there was a well from which gushed oil 'in such abundance that one hundred ships could load it at a time.' The oil, however, was not edible but used for burning and curing scabies, and people traveled from all around to take it away. It lay on the borders of the kingdom of Georgia where the rulers were said to be born with an eagle tattooed on their right shoulder. Georgia was also a region of mountains blocked by Alexander the Great with an iron gate to keep the barbarians from the north out. The Georgians had cities, castles, lovely bolts of silk, and hunting hawks that had no equal. They were Christians and God had blessed them with a lake that filled with fish during Lent but which were not to be seen during the rest of the year.

The Polos turned south and passed the kingdom of Mosul where the muslin was made from silk and gold

47 top The Polo brothers hand the new pope, Gregory X, letters from Kublai, who wanted to learn about Christianity.

47 bottom The nuns in St. Leonard's convent in Georgia receive the ruler of the country, David, who is on the way to a hunt.

thread. In this region there were many Nestorian and Jacobite Christians but also wicked Saracens who robbed merchants. The Venetians survived unharmed and reached the great city of Baghdad where the Caliph lived; Marco commented that the Caliph guided the Saracens like the Pope guided the Christians in Rome. Baghdad is situated on the river Tigris which would take you in eighteen days to a seaport named Bassora (modern Basra) surrounded by groves of date palms from where ships left for India. The artisans in Baghdad produced marvelous clothes decorated with animals and birds, and the Caliph was

reputed to own a tower filled with more gold and silver than had ever been seen at one time. When the Mongol Hulagu Khan (Kublai's brother) took the city in 1255 and captured the Caliph, Hulagu had the Muslim shut up in his treasure house with the instruction to satiate himself on the treasures he loved so much, and in just four days the Caliph was dead from hunger or thirst. And that was the end of the caliphs in Baghdad.

In comparison to its golden era, Baghdad was almost depopulated and its shops rather than its buildings were what was left standing. After looking at the desolation, the three Polos continued on their trip, this time skirting Persia, with its eight kingdoms, many cities, mountains, plains, and sandy deserts so hot it was impossible to camp. The three kings who visited Jesus in the manger traveled from Persia, and in exchange for their gifts, they received a stone that burned with an inextinguishable flame that the Persians still worship. Persia was also the birthplace of the Assassins, whose name was derived from the magical substance, hashish. Their leader was called the 'Old Man of the Mountain' because his castle stood on the peak of Mount Alamut, and he trained his men to murder those he did not like. The manner in which he gulled men to become his assassins was as follows: he would mix hashish with a drink and offer it to his 'guests' who would fall into a deep sleep that would last three days. They would be taken to the castle on the mountain top and placed in a beautiful garden where they would awake to find fountains of wine, and milk and honey, and beautiful girls.

48 top
The Zoroastrian 'Three Kings' set out from Saveh in northern Persia, following the star.

48 bottom
Hulagu locks up the Caliph of Baghdad with his treasure and leaves him to die of hunger.

49 left The Old Man of the Mountain administers the evil potion to three future Assassins.

49 right The Old Man watches pairs of musicians and lovers in his paradise garden.

When they had enjoyed this paradise for a few days, he had them put to sleep once more and then removed from the garden. Wishing to return to paradise, the men were prepared to die so the Old Man of the Mountain sent them into the world to kill and die for the faith, telling them that this was the way to reach paradise. The Assassins had murdered so many people of all faiths that when Hulagu took control of Persia, he decided to destroy them, their organization and their castle once and for all, but the fortress was so strong that the siege lasted three years.

All these things Marco heard from the merchants in the Persian caravan that took the threesome eastward, and he saw Mount Alamut where the castle was no more than a ruin, its fountains dry and its garden overgrown. This and other strange and mar-

of desolate plains, with the occasional halt at oases where the tired and thirsty believed for a while they might be in the Old Man's paradise garden. For example, at Shibarghan, where sweet melons took away one's thirst and hunger and were also sold sliced and dried in the sun. And like Balkh, which the inhabitants boasted was the oldest city in the world and referred to it as the 'mother of all cities.' Another of their claims was that Balkh was where Alexander the Great wanted to marry Statira, the daughter of Darius, king of Persia, but that was more wishful thinking than fact. Balkh, in fact, had suffered a calamity when Genghis Khan destroyed it less than a hundred years before Marco's passing and had everyone he found inside the walls put to death.

Balkh marked the last of the Persian possessions, and when one passed out of it heading east, there

50 Hunters in the region of Badakhshan in Afghanistan about to kill three porcupines.

51 Searching for rubies in Afghanistan. The man on the right offers a red gem to the king of the country.

the area was inhabited by bandits and everyone had retired to live in the ravines in the mountains. However, there was a plentiful water supply and game to catch but, to be sure of surviving, it was necessary to carry enough supplies for both riders and horses.

At the end of this solitary period, the three travelers spied the castle of Taloqan surrounded by pastures, but this was less an area for grazing than for salt-mines as the surrounding mountains consisted of ack salt. It was of cell quality and so hard that

it took a pick to break it. People came from all the surrounding districts to mine it, and were willing to travel up to a month to get there.

Three days farther on, the Venetians came to orchards and vineyards. The farmers that owned them were Muslim and drank wine even if it was forbidden by Mohamed; they were particularly fond of mulled wine and always had a glass to their lips. They dressed from head to foot in animal skins and wound a cord aund thei ad that up to ten spans of the hand in length. Three stages of their journey farther on, the countryside became more inhabited, not only by people but also by porcupines which were good to eat. They were hunted with dogs but the cunning animals would gather together to form a wall of spines. Nor did they restrict themselves to defense but would shoot their spines like darts at the dogs, which withdrew howling.

Three more days of desert crossing followed during which there was nothing to drink or eat before arriving in the province of Badakhshan, which was a vast kingdom whose ruler claimed to be descended from Alexander the Great and Statira, the daughter of Darius, king of Persia. Up until just a short time before Marco's arrival, even the horses were all supposed to have been descended from Alexander's steed, Bucephalus, and were marked with a flash on their foreheads like a sign of equine regality. The story went that the horses were only bred by the uncle of the king but, when the king wanted some, the uncle would not let him have them. In consequence, the king had his uncle killed and, in retribution, the uncle's widow had all the horses burned, thus ending the line of Bucephalus.

In Badakhshan, Niccolò and Maffio Polo found themselves in their element because this was a land of gem mines, in particular of ruby spinel. All the gems were mined from a certain mountain which was the king's property. If anyone set foot on the mountain without permission, his head would be cut off. Other valuables found in this region were lapis lazuli, sapphires and silver. In the mountains thereabouts, there were flocks of hundreds of wild sheep and, however many were captured, there was never any shortage.

It was in this land of mineral wealth that Marco fell ill, perhaps as a result of the climate, perhaps due to the strenuousness of the trip. It was a serious sickness that obliged the Polos to remain there for an entire year until finally someone gave them the right advice: leave the valleys where the air was never free from germs, and head up into the mountains where the air was pure and clean. So they did despite the effort it cost Marco to climb such high peaks, and, once there, he recovered in just a few days.

Thus they could restart their journey, all of them richer for their halt: Niccolò and Maffio because they had bought gems advantageously, and Marco because he had spent his time learning Persian and Mongolian. They three followed the course of the Amu Darya and rose ever higher in the mountains which Marco had heard were the tallest in the world. They saw no birds because birds were not capable of flying in such thin air, and the flames of their fires gave no warmth as the air was so cold. And yet people lived there, wild and wicked, who wore animal skins and seemed like animals themselves. But up on the Pamir plateau where the three marched for twelve days, no-one lived at all; there were no houses, not even a blade of grass.

YULE's MAP

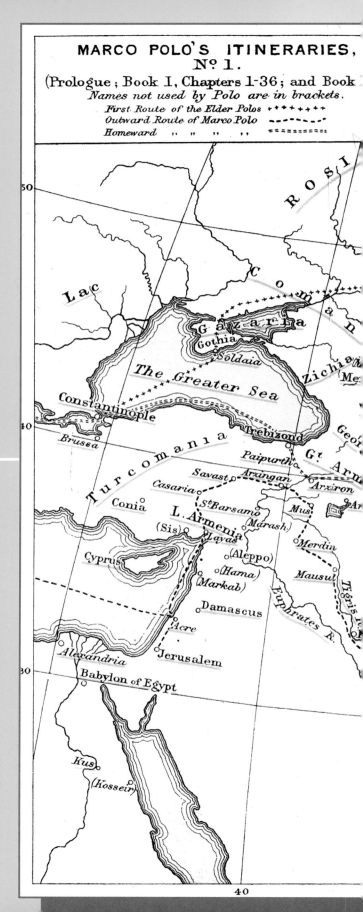

MARCO POLO'S ITINERARIES,
Nº 1.
(Prologue ; Book I, Chapters 1-36 ; and Book
Names not used by Polo are in brackets.
First Route of the Elder Polos
Outward Route of Marco Polo
Homeward   "   "   "   "

SIR HENRY YULE'S BOOK, '*THE TRAVELS OF MARCO POLO*', WAS FIRST PUBLISHED IN 1870 and is unquestionably the best and most exhaustive analysis of the Venetian's journey. Each passage of *Il Milione* is considered critically and commented by a variety of ancient and contemporary authors. In consequence, the maps created from this mass of detail are still the most reliable on the subject.

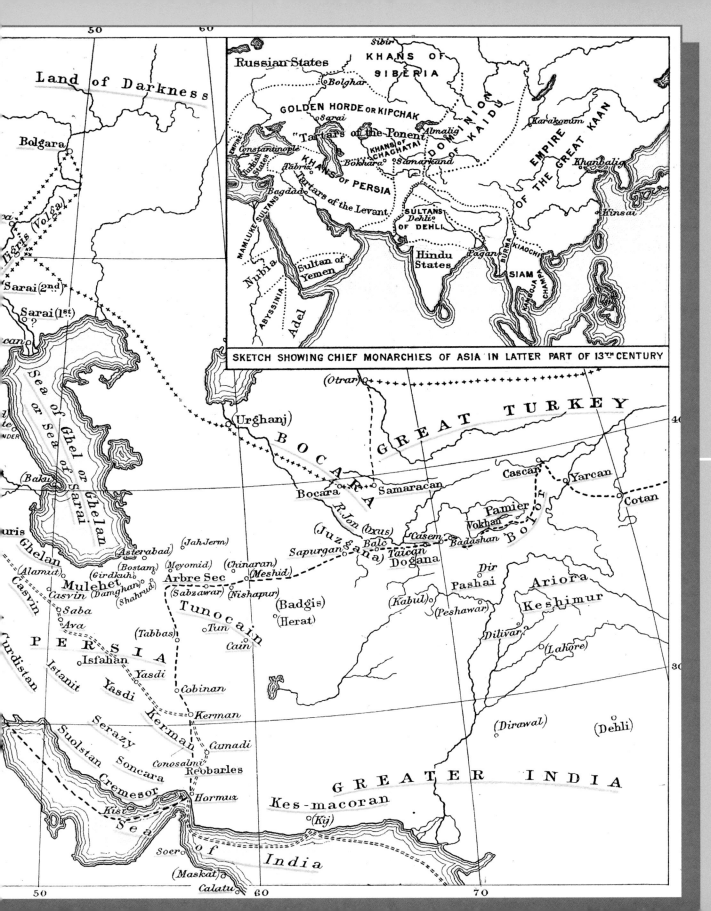

Land of Darkness

Bolgara

Tigris (Volga)

Sarai (2nd)

Sarai (1st)

Sea of Ghel or Sea of Sarai

(Baku)

Ghelan

Turkish States

PERSIA

Kurdistan

Istanit

Casvin

Mulehet

Casvin

(Alamut)

(Damghan)

Saba

Ava

(Tabbas)

Isfahan

Yasdi

Serazy

Suolstan

Soncara

Cremesor

Kisi

Soer

Sea of

(Maskat)

Calatu

India

Kerman

Cobinan

Cumadi

Conosalmi

Reobarles

Hormuz

Kes-macoran

(Kij)

GREATER INDIA

(Dirawal)

(Dehli)

Lahore

Dilivar

Keshimur

Ariora

Pashai

Dir

(Kabul)

(Peshawar)

Badgis

(Herat)

Tunocain

Tun

Cain

(Sabzawar)

(Nishapur)

Arbre Sec

(Meshid)

(Chinaran)

(Meyomid)

(Bostam)

(Girdkuh)

Shahrud

Asterabad

(JahJerm)

Sapurgan

(Juzgana)

Dogana

Taican

Balc

Casem

Badashan

Vokhan

Pamier

B O L O R

Cascar

Yarcan

Cotan

R.Jon (Oxus)

Bocara

Samaracan

BOCARA

GREAT TURKEY

(Urghanj)

(Otrar)

Russian States

Sibir

KHANS OF SIBERIA

Bolghar

GOLDEN HORDE OR KIPCHAK

Sarai

"Tartars of the Ponent

Almalig

Karakorum

DOMINION OF KAIDU

EMPIRE OF THE GREAT KAAN

KHANS OF CHAGHATAI

Constantinople

Turkish States

EMPIRE

Bokhara

Samarkand

Khanbalig

Tabriz

KHANS OF PERSIA

Bagdad

Tartars of the Levant

SULTANS Dehli OF DEHLI

Kinsai

MAMLUKE SULTANS

Nubia

Sultan of Yemen

ABYSSINIA

Adel

Hindu States

Pagan

BURMA

KIAOCHI

SIAM

CAMBOJA

CHAMPA

MICHAEL YAMASHITA

VENICE

V ENICE IS ONE OF THE MOST
EXTRAORDINARY PLACES IN THE WORLD,
WHERE LAND AND SEA MEET TO CREATE A
CITY WHERE BY RIGHTS THERE SHOULD BE
ONLY WATER.

It is a city of surprises, where one encounters beauty and wonder around every corner, a place where the past can still be witnessed as part of everyday life. But Venice's charms also make it one of the most difficult subjects for a photographer. Perhaps the most photographed city in the world, it is a challenge to capture its sense of living history in a way that hasn't been tried before, by hundreds of photographers, from every angle and in every light imaginable.

Our goal was to evoke the atmosphere of the city on the sea in which Marco grew up. On the surface, this seemed an easy task, as the alleyways, palaces, canals and squares of Venice have changed little in seven centuries. The city today teems with people who have come from all over the planet, just as in the time of Marco Polo, when it was a cosmopolitan city of seamen and merchants, when the canals we see today were filled with faces from every nation, wearing gems from India and Ceylon, with

swords forged in Tabriz, with gold jewelry worked in Persia, and with silks from remotest Asia.

We began by shooting the places most directly associated with Marco Polo. The first stop was the Cannaregio neighborhood where his home, the "Corte del Milione," was located. His contemporary Venetians nicknamed him Marco "Milione," perhaps after the "millions" of marvels he described, the millions of whoppers he might have told or the millions of lira earned from the treasures the Polos brought back to Venice. After shooting the house in the quiet courtyard marked only by a small plaque, our next destination was the Grand Canal.

Despite the fact the buildings along the canal convey an aura of Marco's day, the bulk of the traffic on the Grand Canal comes not from picturesque gondolas, but from modern water-taxis, ferries plowing up and down the waterway, and working boats loaded with goods and produce.

The one exception is during the Regatta Storico, a celebration of Venice's maritime history. The September spectacle features only gondolas. After a day of races, hundreds of small

A BRIDGE TO
THE PAST

55 A palace in Cannaregi
is reflected in the lagoon

spectators' boats follow in the wake of the last gondola and gather in the center of the canal. We decided to return for Regatta weekend.

To take what might seem a simple snapshot of a boating event actually took precision planning. I had scouted a "room with a view," and reserved a suite with a balcony in the Rialto Hotel overlooking the canal and the Rialto Bridge. On the day of the race, I hired a gondola to take me up and down the canal so that I could photograph any boats that seemed to me particularly striking but, by the end of the competition, I had not gotten anything I was satisfied with. It was dusk when the gondolier finally dropped me at the steps of the Rialto Bridge, and I realized I was about to lose my light. I ran up the steps to the hotel and raced back to my room. I opened the window and saw Venice at twilight, with the last gondola in the race coming up the canal. As soon as it passed, all the boats headed for the center of the canal on cue, and I got the frame I was looking for.

I've always said photographers are paid to be lucky, and that weekend proved no exception. My next challenge in Venice was to find a novel way to shoot the Piazza San Marco, with the familiar view of the Ducal Palace, the Biblioteca Marciana and the two columns on the quay. This was the view of the square that Marco would have seen on the day he left Venice for China. By happy coincidence, I found out that the world's largest cruise ship was about to enter Venice. If I could get the timing right, and find the right angle, I could juxtapose this symbol of the modern world against the Square's solitary towers as it sailed by on the Grand Canal.

Early on the morning of September 6, my assistant Marisa Montibeller and I headed out for San Marco loaded with my equipment and carrying a ten-foot long ladder to shoot above the heads of the tourists feeding pigeons in the square. When we found our location, I positioned two cameras with brackets on the top of the ladder. I left Marisa to watch for the ship which was due to arrive at 10 o'clock sharp while I moved to the foot of the campanile to set up for another view. We were all set when the police arrived just before 10. They questioned Marisa, asking what she was doing and if she had a permit to set up all the equipment in the square. She calmly called me on her cell phone and said, "The police want to move me out of the square, Michael." "Don't move. Stay where you are as long as you possibly can," I shouted. Marisa, who is not only efficient but also resourceful, used her charm to stall the police with a discussion of the matter for about ten minutes. The ship had still not arrived, but just as the police had run out of patience and were about to shoo Marisa away, the *Grand Princess* glided into view. She was immense, and everyone on the square, amazed by her size, turned to watch. The ship sailed majestically past St. Mark's, sending the square's famed pigeons swooping into the air. That was the frame.

Venice can be a difficult city to work in, especially when hauling camera bags, not to mention ten-foot ladders, on foot, up steps, over bridges and across canals, but the effort is often repaid with the perfect setting or subject. For example, there was the day I met a young sailor, who took me around the canals for a whole day on his vegetable boat. His right arm was completely covered in Chinese-inspired tatoos - a stroke of photographer's luck, as Marco had written at length about the Chinese custom of tattooing, unheard of in Venice seven hundred years ago. Another example of our good fortune was the lucky find discovered in the Cannaregio, Marco's old neighborhood - a detail on a building of a Venetian merchant with a camel, which became the lead picture of the National Geographic story on Marco.

The ebb and flow of the sea up, around and through Venice makes for a city that is constantly changing, depending on the season or time of day. But one of her greatest ironies is that however much the city changes, the past is always a presence in Venice. And so is Marco Polo. As his tales of exotic travels became widely known, the work of cartographers and historians in the centuries that followed continued to be influenced by his book. I was gratified to learn that the venerable *mappa mundi*, the "map of the world," drawn by Fra Mauro in the 15th century and housed in Venice's Biblioteca, laid out the nations of the world just as Marco Polo stated. This same geographic configuration was repeated in countless later maps and books. Though Marco's influence is remarkable, even more remarkable was the casual way in which the *mappa mundi*, a six-hundred year old work of art and science, is displayed. When I asked to see it, the curator simply whisked back the curtain behind his desk to reveal the map, framed but unprotected by glass or security monitors. But that's the way it is in Venice: The past is not a novelty. Italians are accustomed to living with their past every day. I saw it often, glancing over the side of a bridge, or off the quay, photographing watery images of Venice reflected in the mirror of time.

THE CANNAREGIO
QUARTER
THE ANCESTRAL ROOTS
OF THE POLOS

"For ye shall find therein all kinds of wonderful things, and the divers histories of the Great Hermenia, and of Persia, and of the Land of the Tartars, and of India, and of many other country of which our Book doth speak."

The Travels of Marco Polo, *Prologue.*

58-59 A camel and merchant are immortalized on the façade of a palace in Cannaregio.

60 The Polos' house probably faced onto the
thirteenth-century Corte del Milione.

61 The sea confines and defines the city of Venice,
making it unique.

62-63 The *Grand Princess* appears in the setting of
St. Mark's Square.

TWILIGHT IN VENICE
LIGHTS AND SHADOWS ON THE "CALLE"

64-65 Berthed at a quay, boats are harbored
after a hectic day.

66 A silk cloth showing the Polo family crest.

67 The map of the world drawn by Fra Mauro was based on
the information provided in *The Travels of Marco Polo*.

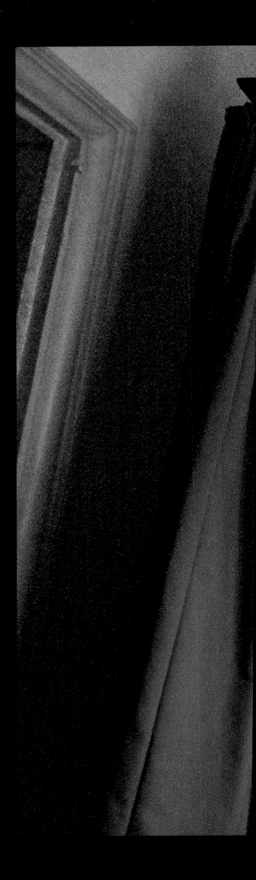

St. Mark's Square:
A last look at Venice

*"The crowd of the people that you meet here
at all hours, passing this way and that on
their different errands, is so vast that no one
would believe it possible that victuals enough
could be provided for their consumption."*

The Travels of Marco Polo, *Vol. II, Bk. 2, Ch. 77*

68-69 A deserted St. Mark's Square: as rare
today as it was in Marco Polo's lifetime.

70-71 During the Regatta, the canals are
crowded with traditional gondolas.

IRAQ

———◆———

A JOURNEY ON THE SILK ROAD TODAY, WITH ALL-TERRAIN VEHICLES, HIGH-TECH NAVIGATIONAL GEAR AND COMMUNICATIONS EQUIPMENT, COULD THEORETICALLY TAKE A COUPLE OF MONTHS. IN PRACTICE, HOWEVER, IT IS IMPOSSIBLE: THERE ARE TOO MANY ONGOING WARS IN THE TERRITORY BETWEEN EUROPE AND CHINA.

In Marco's day, it took years of traveling by horse, donkey and camel caravan. While Marco had only one empire to cross, we, in 1999, had many and were unable even to get halfway. During Marco Polo's lifetime, the power of Kublai Khan and his Mongol horsemen stretched from China's Pacific coast to the gates of the West in eastern Europe, spreading his influence and empire 4,400 miles across Asia. Today that area is broken up into nations and people in conflict with one another. Along his way, Marco received various forms of green lights, easing his passage through Mongol territories. In Acre, in what is today Israel and during Marco's time, a stronghold of western Crusaders, he was issued a pass of safe-conduct by the Pope, who asked that he carry a message from the Catholic Church to the Mongol conqueror, who had expressed intentions to convert to Chris-

tianity. Once he reached Asia, Marco was given a paiza, that allowed travelers to move freely across borders.

Though we had equipment to get us over physical borders, political boundaries proved much tougher to cross. Turkey, Iraq, Iran and Afghanistan all have closed or restricted borders. Receiving permission to enter Iraq was our first hurdle. It was not an easy one as direct relations between Iraq and the United States were practically ceased between the two Gulf Wars, and journalists, especially American journalists, were rarely welcomed. We explained that the purpose of our trip was to research and photograph sites for our story on Marco Polo and that we had no political agenda. The Iraqi ambassador must have been convinced, since we were issued a two month visa, our own paiza. Once in Iraq, we turned, as we would so often on this journey, to Marco's account of his travels. His exact route through Iraq is not entirely clear; nonetheless, he provides surprisingly accurate information on travel through the country. He arrived in what is now Iraq with little idea of who the barbarous people inhabiting the land were, nor had he ever seen an oil well. He became the first European to describe one, a natu-

The gold of Baghdad

73 At dawn, worshippers enter Khadimain Mosque in Baghdad

tal well not far from Mount Ararat and the Caspian Sea in what is now Azerbaijan. He said the oozing liquid is "not good to use with food but 'is' good to burn" oblivious to the importance that this "black gold" was to have in the future.

He also spoke of the Kurds in what is now northern Iraq, calling them bandits who preyed on merchants and a warlike people who never parted with their weapons. Once again, Marco's seven-hundred-year old descriptions sound completely modern. Though they may no longer be "bandits," many Kurds, both men and women, go about their daily routines with AK-47s slung over their shoulders, whether they are grazing their animals or celebrating a wedding. We witnessed this at a marriage ceremony in Jundian in Iraqi Kurdistan, where a group of lovely young women looked like blushing bridesmaids except for the machine guns worn over their party finery. Though the Kurds of Marco's day may indeed have raided caravans, Iraqi Kurds live in conditions that justify bearing arms. War is a fact of life for them.

One disconcerting aspect of this constant upheaval is the presence of countless land mines throughout Kurdistan. We met a few Westerners — mostly Australians and New Zealanders — who, under the auspices of the United Nations, seek out and deactivate the mines hidden below the thin layer of fertile prairies and grazing lands.

I photographed one of these missions in Choman, in an area of gently rolling meadows overlooked by distant mountains. It is a landscape bathed by pure, vigorous air, but stopping to savor the magnificent and peaceful scenery could cost you your life if you step past the slender wire that marks the boundary of the safe meadows. I discovered that even stopping by the road for a picture can be dangerous, as one step off the asphalt onto the grass might mean setting off a mine. These hidden threats make such fertile land completely unusable.

Near Kurdistan, lies Mosul, situated in the heart of ancient Mesopotamia on the Tigris River. As Marco describes it, it was a center of religion and commerce. The Venetian tells of large communities of Moslem Arabs, Nestorian Christians and members of the Jacobite Church. In Mosul, Marco found "mosulin," a locally produced cotton trimmed with gold and silken thread, which is still one of the area's most precious commodities. He also writes of gold, pearls and spices, which were of as much value to the medieval West as any gems.

While Marco must have had relatively open access to these areas, armed with his paiza, we were constantly accompanied by official "minders," erstwhile guides supplied by the government. On most assignments, a photographer works with a "fixer," a local who makes arrangements and reservations, obtains permissions and generally makes sure we have what we need to get the best possible pictures. A minder's goal i to make sure we get the stories or pictures that show a locale only in the ways the government wants to be seen.

One afternoon, I wanted to photograph from the top of Al Hadba minaret of the great Nuraddin Mosque, which was built in the thirteenth century and almost certainly seen by Marco, but my implacable minder was determined not to let me photograph anything which, in his opinion, the government would not have authorized. As I later found out, he was most worried that I might shoot a military installation or one of palaces that belonged then to Saddam Hussein. He finally allowed me to climb to the top just to have a look. I charged ahead, quickly climbing up the narrow, twisted stairway that led to the top. Half way up the tower, I suddenly realized that my guide was not behind me. It seems that he suffered from claustrophobia and was experiencing a severe case of it in the cramped stairwell below. Without looking back, I climbed to the top and began shooting. I photographed the expanse of courtyards, low houses, porticoes and the occasional dome of the flat city of Mosul, a place virtually unchanged since the thirteenth century. By the time my guide made his tortured way up to meet me, I had all the pic-

tures I needed. As he caught his breath, I grinned and reported that I hadn't seen anything of interest and was ready to head back down.

Heading south, Marco describes Baghdad (Baudas to Marco) as the equivalent in the East to Rome in the West, and compares the Caliph, the title of the spiritual successor to Mohammed and the leader and spiritual guide of Moslems around the world, to the Pope. As it was impossible to reach Baghdad without infringing on the no-fly zone imposed by the United Nations after the Gulf War to protect the Shiites and Kurds who had been slaughtered en masse by the Iraqis, we had to travel ten hours overland from Jordan, where we crossed the same bare, monotonous desert wastelands that Marco had traveled through into the palm fringed "Fertile Crescent" of the Tigris and Euphrates rivers.

Baghdad, a city of modern sand-colored buildings, is known as the city of mosques and is distinguished by domes, of which there were two principal types: those built to glorify Allah and those used to mask the miseries of war with glory. At dawn, the gold of the domes of Khadimain Mosque ignite, moving both the faithful and the visitor with the elegance and natural balance of Islamic architecture. By evening, the blue half-domes of the Martyrs Shrine war memorial that commemorates the one million Iraqis who fell in the battle against Iran (from 1980 to 1988) cast-ed an eerie glow across the city. Ironically, today that awful monument to useless wars lies inside a military base belonging to the occupying forces. No Iraqi can, or probably ever will be allowed to set foot there. But its shadow still falls.

Then, in Baghdad, the presence of Saddam Hussein was inescapable. Venerated like a Caliph of the past, his picture was hanging in every office and public place. And a mosaic portrait of one of Iraq's staunchest enemies, George Bush, with the words "Bush is Criminal" used to decorate the floor at the entrance of the Al Rashid Hotel, where many official foreign visitors and VIPs were housed, making it impossible to enter or leave without walking on the face of Saddam's nemesis.

Hoping to get a picture of the mysterious and elusive Iraqi leader, we went to a birthday celebration for Saddam in his birthplace of Tikrit. A gigantic cake, iced in pink and green, floated like an island in the midst of a sea of TV crews, officials, and military personnel who thronged the square. Though the guest of honor never showed, I tried to at least get a picture of the immense cake, but found myself being pushed further and further forward by the crowds until my stomach was squashed into the creamy mass. In the end, the closest I came to Saddam Hussein was when I posed beside his smiling image on a propaganda poster. Marco wrote of the many artifacts of the area that were prized for their quality, especially the local carpets, so before leaving Iraq, I hoped

to buy a souvenir for my daughter. However, the embargo that had shattered the economy of Iraq made it illegal to export items from the country. Even if I had been able to find a carpet to purchase, it would have been confiscated at Customs. In the end, I found a small rug, printed not with tribal patterns or intricate designs, but Mickey Mouse. I figured a Disney character wouldn't raise too many eyebrows at U.S. Customs, though Saddam would probably not have been thrilled to know that my one memento of his country was such a prominent symbol of his arch-enemy. Perhaps the reason the Iraqis were willing to have us stay for two months was their hope that we would report on the impoverished conditions there, helping to lift some of the world sanctions that have crippled the economy of Iraq. Yet, despite the poverty, children played in the streets of cities like Basra – streets lined by splendid but now dilapidated buildings dating to the times of Marco Polo – unaware that within a few years the price of freedom would have been paid and all would be different. And our ever-present official watchdogs notwithstanding, we found the Iraqis to be a friendly people who are happy to talk, people who did not even realize that they are seen as an enemy of the West. But ironically, we discovered that most Iraqis had never heard of the man who first brought tales of the former glories of their culture back to the West seven hundred years ago. But Iraq, as we know, is not China! .

IRAQ

MOSUL

Tigris

TIKRIT
SAMARRA

BAGHDAD

Euphrates

BASRA

TOWARD THE
HORMUZ STRAITS

- ● City visited or described

- ● Other major sites

- •••••••• Outward route

0   93 Miles

RUWANDUZ
GATEWAY TO THE SILK ROAD

78 A Kurd village almost merges with the landscape in north-east Iraq.

79 Ruwanduz stands in the ancient homelands of the Kurds.

The mountains of the Kurds

"There is yet another race of people who inhabit the mountains in that quarter, and are called Curds. Some of them are Christians, and some of them are Saracens; but they are an evil generation, whose delight it is to plunder merchants."

The Travels of Marco Polo, *Vol. I, Bk. 1, Ch. 5*

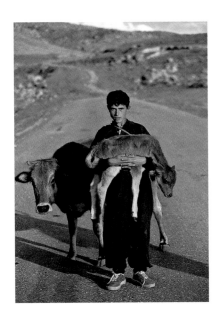

80 With his AK-47 in hand, a Kurd shepherd leads his flock to pasture.

81 A young Kurd shepherd holds up the newest addition to the flock.

Spring comes to Kurdistan

"In this country there are many cruel and murderous people, so that no day passes but there is some homicide among them. Were it not for the Government, which is that of the Tartars of the Levant, they would do great mischief to merchants; and indeed, maugre the government, they often succeed in doing such mischief."

The Travels of Marco Polo, *Vol. I, Bk. 1, Ch. 15*

82-83 Kurds celebrate Nawruz, the festival of spring, on the Little Zab, a tributary of the Tigris.

A Kurdish wedding

5 A wedding in Jundian: flakes of
foam rain down on the newly-weds.

BAGHDAD
CITY OF DOMES

"Now it came to pass on a day in the year of Christ 1255, that the Lord of the Tartars of the Levant, whose name was Alaü [...] gathered a mighty host and came up against Baudas and took it by storm. It was a great enterprise! for in Baudas there were more than 100,000 horse, besides foot soldiers."

The Travels of Marco Polo, *Vol. I, Bk. 1, Ch. 6*

90-91 The double dome in Baghdad dedicated to the dead during the war against Iran, which today lies in a military base off-limits to Iraqis.

"There was a Calif at Baudas who bore a great hatred to Christians, and was taken up day and night with the thought how he might bring those that were in his kingdom over to his own faith."

The Travels of Marco Polo, *Vol. I, Bk. 1, Ch. 7*

BAGHDAD

ROME OF THE SARACENS

92 A devotee kisses the door of Khadimain Mosque.

93 At dawn, Khadimain Mosque is shown in its full splendor.

86-87 Despite the happy occasion,
war is never over for these wedding
guests in Jundian.

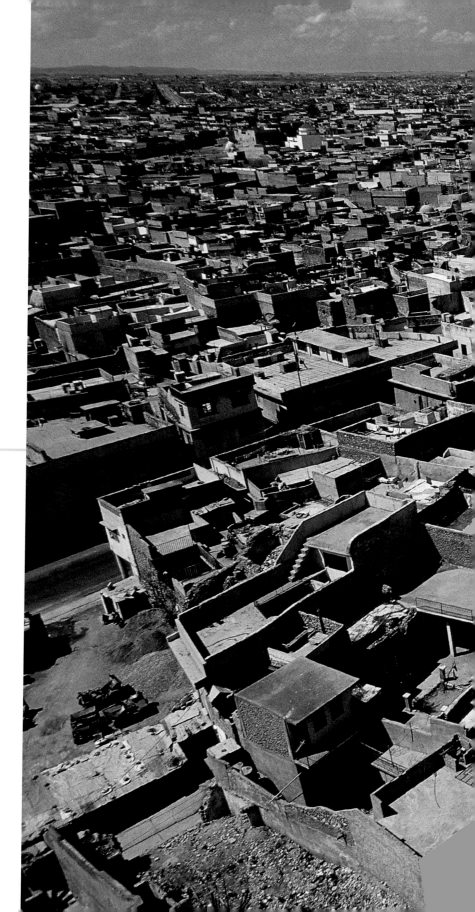

MOSUL
THE MUSLIN CITY

"All the clothes of gold and silk that are called Mosolins are made in this country; and those great Merchants called Mosolins, who carry for sale such quantities of spicery and pearls and clothes of silk and gold, are also from this kingdom."

The Travels of Marco Polo, *Vol. I, Bk. 1, Ch. 5*

88-89 The expanse of low buildings in Mosul cannot have changed much since Marco's time.

Ramadan in Baghdad
The month of penitence

94-95 In the Fourteenth Ramadan Mosque, the
faithful prostrate themselves. It is Friday, the
Moslem holy day.

96 A two-hour service tests the devotion of the youngest members of this Nestorian congregation.

97 Christian children pray in a home for impoverished families in Baghdad.

BAGHDAD
THE TAILORS' BAZAAR

"In Baudas they have many different kinds of silk stuffs and gold brocades, such as nasich, and nac and cramoisy, and many another beautiful tissue richly wrought with figures of beastes and birds.
It is the noblest and greatest city in all those regions."

The Travels of Marco Polo, *Vol. I, Bk. 1, Ch. 6*

98-99 Trying on a new garment in the Al Saati market in Baghdad: the *abah* must fall perfectly.

100 In a market in Baghdad, copper pots being repaired are beaten and soldered on small anvils stuck in the ground.

Baghdad

Life goes on after the war

101 An improvised and streamlined swing.

THE GOLD OF THE TIGRIS

"A very great river flows through the city, [...].
There is a great traffic of merchants with their
goods this way; they descend some eighteen
days [...] and then come to a certain city called
Kisi, where they enter the Sea of India."

The Travels of Marco Polo, *Vol. 1, Bk. 1, Ch. 6*

102-103 Gold-hunters sieve the river for
waste from the nearby goldsmiths' souk.

Baghdad
In the Fertile Crescent

104-105 Harvesting parsley in a suburban area of the city of Baghdad.

"Now I have told you something of Baudas. I could easily indeed have told you first of the affairs and the customs of the people there. But it would be too long a business, looking to the great and strange things that I have got to tell you."

The Travels of Marco Polo, *Vol. I, Bk. 1, Ch. 10*

106-107 A group of dervishes celebrates the 62nd birthday of Saddam Hussein in Tikrit.

THE PRESIDENT'S
BIRTHDAY

108 and 109 Everyone was celebrating in Tikrit but that day the guest of honor did not show up for the festivities.

110-111 Children's games beneath the magnificent spiral minaret in Samarra, 1100 years old.

Basra

"The largest city in all the regions"

112 In the Old City the traditional architecture crumbles from neglect.

113 Skipping rope in the ancient Arab quarter of Ashar in Basra.

The Marsh Arabs
Reed houses

❖

114-115 Life in a traditional communal house built from lake reeds north of Basra. The design of the Marsh Arabs' houses is thousands of years old.

IRAN

IRAN IS THE FIRST PLACE ANYONE WHO HAS DOUBTS ABOUT MARCO'S CLAIMS SHOULD VISIT. MARCO POLO'S DESCRIPTIONS OF THE LAND AND PEOPLE OF PERSIA, AS HE WOULD HAVE KNOWN IT, ARE SO ACCURATE AND, IN MANY CASES, SO CURRENT, THAT THEY ARE ASTONISHING.

Marco crossed Persia on two occasions about twenty years apart: on his journey to China and on his return to Europe. On the outbound leg of his trip he most likely traveled by sea from Basra in the extreme south of Iraq to Hormuz, and from there went north towards Bam and Kerman, then further on, to what is now modern Afghanistan. On his journey home across Persia he landed in Hormuz and headed north, to Yazd, then to Qazvin, Tabriz and the present day Turkish border When he entered Persia, he found himself at the edge of an immense territory, crossed diagonally by the "backbone" of the Zagros mountains. The mountains, then as now, dominated the geography of the country, as well as the layout of its roads, most of which ran from the north-west to the south-east. We followed the same route, beginning from the Persian city that was the last that Marco visited: Tabriz, known to Marco as Tauris. Tabriz was

famous among Italian merchants of the thirteenth century for its precious stones, gold and silk and for the refined beauty of the jewelry sold in its Bazaar, the richest market in the Middle East. The Bazaar, little changed over the centuries and one of the few ancient buildings to have survived the earthquakes that regularly strike the area, is just as Marco described it, with some of the best carpets, silks and gold jewelry available in the region. Tabriz, far away from the barren deserts of southeast Iran, was and is still renowned for its fruit which was, as Marco commented, "large and excellent." Between Tabriz and Teheran, we were on the lookout for Mount Alamut, the Mountain of the Assassins, hoping to find some remnant of the heavenly gardens it was once known for. In ancient Persia, the "Old Man of the Mountain," as he was known, lived in a palace there during his reign of terror. To dispose of his enemies, he would gull young men into committing murder for him by serving them an elixir of hashish (from which the term assassin stems) that sent them into a coma-like sleep for three days, after which they awoke in the Old Man's paradise gardens, where they, thinking they must surely be in heaven, feasted on bread and honey, wine, more hashish and beautiful young women. The Old Man

VEILED FAITH

Tabriz
The carpet market

then sent them away, but promised that if they complied with his orders to kill his enemies, even if they died in the attempt, they could come back to his Eden as martyrs. However, all we found of the Assassins' earthly Eden was an archaeological excavation site, nothing but large holes in the ground, dug by scholars trying to piece together the remains of the 13th century palace. The road that crosses the country took us into the heart of Iran, leading to the magnificent city of Yazd that so much impressed Marco. With the knowledgeable eye of a merchant, Marco describes the manufacture of the splendid *yazdi*, a silk cloth embroidered with gold thread that is still produced here. Marco was also impressed by the engineering feats he found in Yazd. For example, he described the water supply system, still in use today, provided by the *qanat*, tunnels that transported water from the mountains to create an oasis in a landscape of monotonous desert. Marco was intrigued, too, by Yazd's Towers of the Wind, which at first glance might seem to be minarets. In fact, these slender, four- or more sided structures are ancient and remarkably efficient home air conditioners. The towers house ducts that draw air in through grates on the lower floors where it is cooled and humidified by running through tanks of water before rising to displace the hot (and therefore lighter) air in the houses above. The hot exhaust then exits from the grates in the upper part of the tower, leaving

the interiors of the house fresh and cool, in contrast to the blistering, dry air outside. The view today from one of Yazd's minarets in the soft light of dawn or dusk, of the Towers of the Wind rising from the expanse of low, sand-colored buildings and domes lined with tiles of a blue that add a refreshing coolness to the thirsty landscape, is nearly the same one that so struck Marco, straight out of *A Thousand and One Nights*. As he made his way through Persia, Marco paid increasing attention to the religions with which he came into contact. Iran has not officially been a Moslem country for long. Prior to the 1979 revolution that toppled secular power and replaced it with fundamentalist Muslim rule, Iran was governed by a shah who claimed to be the descendant of the ancient Persian emperors Darius and Cyrus. During Marco's time in Persia, Christian sects were quite numerous. Marco speaks of communities of Georgian, Nestorian, Jacobite and Armenian Christians who all inhabited different zones of Yazd. Marco also refers to Zoroastrianism, the monotheistic faith that was the national religion of Persia 600 years before the establishment of Christianity and 1200 years before the establishment of Islam. Today there are still communities of "fire worshippers" as Marco called them; near Yazd I photographed one of their ancient Towers of Silence, where the dead were placed on circular open platforms and left to be eaten by birds of prey in a ceremony referred to as Sky Burial. Following Marco Polo's trail across Persia, we arrived at Bam, an impressive ghost city circled by immense "earth walls," which Marco described in his book. The walls were made with the only materials at hand in that ruthlessly bare terrain, mud and straw, which insulated the walls of the public and domestic buildings from the heat. Bam is a silent relic of the past, but just outside this lonely abandoned city there is plenty of life. Today the silence is even greater. Bam no longer exists: on 26 December 2003 the Earth's destructive power brought down the fragile walls that had resisted man and nature for centuries, killing 40,000 people. There is no longer anything except the vestige of ancient vestiges; the citadel lies in ruins but will be reconstructed, thanks to an international project already underway. The reconstruction represents a faith in the positive aspects of humanity which, it must be hoped, will spread throughout the Middle East. We next set out to find the hot springs Marco described, which were south of Bam. Marco spoke of finding water that was "good for curing many infirmities." He was referring to the springs of Cheshme Genu not far from the coast and still known today for their properties. When we asked the locals where we might find the healing waters, they sent us to a valley of rocks and low shrubs. There we found a remarkable stream. Its sulfurous water is filled with copper which makes it such a

bright green that it seems like a vein of phosphorescent emerald, a surprising jewel springing from the earth, and still a popular place for soothing soaks. Our last destination in Persia was the Strait of Hormuz. The people who live along the coast of the Persian Gulf do not seem to have changed much since the Middle Ages. Photographing the men and women in Minab, I found the same dark-skinned Moslems (descendants of African slaves) that Marco had described in the region. Today and for centuries before Marco's arrival, the women have covered their faces with the *hejab*, the red mask that reveals only their black, glittering eyes — like the visor on a medieval helmet. Once they reached Hormuz, Marco, his father and uncle had intended to embark for India. With the expert knowledge of ships that came with being the citizens of a powerful seafaring republic, they sized up the local boats known as dhows, deemed them unseaworthy and decided to give up on their plan to cross the Arabian Sea. Marco and company were obliged to turn back and continue their epic journey to China by land. We also arrived on the Gulf coast looking for boats, not to sail in, but to photograph. But instead of Arab dhows, all we found were fiberglass motor boats. But, at the magic hour of dusk, by photographing them in silhouette, I was able to make a picture that both evoked the past and hid the present.

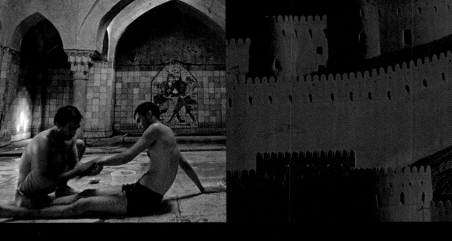

IRAN

TABRIZ

ALAMAT

TEHERAN

ARBRE SEC
(SABZEVAR)

YAZD

ISFAHAN

KERMAN

BAM

BANDAR I
ABBAS

MINAB

STRAIT OF HORMUZ

- ● City visited or described
- ● Other major sites
- ●●●● Outward route
- ●●●● Homeward route

0   217 Miles

Kandovan

Ancient and unchanged

122 Two weavers take a break in one of the ancient houses in Kandovan.

123 Still inhabited, the ancient houses in Kandovan are dug out of
cones of eroded rock.

TABRIZ
THE GOLD
AND JEWELRY MARKET

"Tauris attracts many Latin merchants, especially Genoese, to buy goods and transact other business there; the more as it is also a great market for precious stones."

The Travels of Marco Polo, *Vol. I, Bk. 1, Ch. 11*

124-125 The bazaar in Tabriz is still famous for its jewelry and gold and silver ornaments.

126-127 Gazorkhan perches at the feet of the Assassins' Castle, south of the Caspian.

The Towers of Silence
Burial places of the Zoroastrians

128 In Yazd, the Towers of Silence were open-air burial places.

129 Votive chapels at the base of the Zoroastrian funerary platforms.

Yazd

Good and noble city

"The heat is tremendous, and on that account their houses are built with ventilators to catch the wind. These ventilators are placed on the side from which the wind comes, and they bring the wind down into the house to cool it. But for this the heat would be utterly unbearable."

The Travels of Marco Polo, *Vol. II, Bk. 3, Ch. 40*

130-131 Yazd bristles with dozens of Towers of the Wind.

Yazd
Jame Masjid

132-133 The Jame Masjid (Friday Mosque)
is a masterpiece of elegant polychromy.

Yazd

A pearl in the desert

134-135 Sunset inflames the crescent
symbol atop the dome of the Jame Masjid.

"*Kerman is a kingdom which is properly in Persia, and formerly it had a hereditary prince. Since the Tartars conquered the country the rule is no longer hereditary, but the Tartars sends to administer whatever lord he pleases.*"

The Travels of Marco Polo, *Vol. I, Bk. 1, Ch. 17*

136-137 One of Kerman's oldest hammams, (Turkish baths) still in use today.

138-139 Mighty Bam was built by the Zoroastrians in the twelfth century.

ANCIENT BAM
"THE DESERT OF THE TARTARS"

"In this plain there are a number of villages and towns which have lofty walls of mud, made as a defence against the banditti, who are very numerous, and are called Caraonas. This name is given them because they are the sons of Indian mothers by Tartar fathers."

The Travels of Marco Polo, *Vol. I, Bk. 1, Ch. 18*

140-141 Destroyed by a dreadful earthquake in 2003, Bam – once the largest citadel in the world – will be reconstructed by an international project.

The emerald springs

*"On the road by which we return from
Hormos to Kerman you meet with some
very fine plains, and you also find many
natural hot baths. [...] The baths that I
have mentioned have excellent virtues;
they cure the itch and several other
diseases."*

The Travels of Marco Polo, *Vol. I, Bk. 1, Ch. 19*

142-143 Rich with copper, the sulfurous water in
Cheshme Genu is effective against skin diseases.

THE EMBROIDERY OF TIME
THE ART OF SILK AND GOLD

145

"The ladies of the country and their daughters also produce exquisite needlework in the embroidery of silk stuffs in different colours, with figures of beasts and birds, trees and flowers, and a variety of other patterns."

The Travels of Marco Polo, *Vol. I, Bk. I, Ch. 17*

144-145 A girl embroiders fine silk with gold thread.

Bandar i Abbas
The gateway to India

146-147 Traditional fishing in the Strait of Hormuz, off Bandar i Abbas.

"The residents avoid living in the cities, for the heat in summer is so great that it would kill them. Hence they go out to sleep [...] where there are streams and plenty of water. [...] When they perceive that wind coming they plunge into water up to the neck, and so abide until the wind has ceased."

The Travels of Marco Polo, *Vol. I, Bk. 1, Ch. 19*

148-149 In this extreme tip of Iran, the wind and water provide a comfort the interior lacks.

THE PERSIAN GULF
A SEA OF MERCHANTS
AND PIRATES

"Their ships are wretched affairs, and many of them get lost; for they have no iron fastenings, and are only stitched together with twine made from the husk of the Indian nut."

The Travels of Marco Polo, *Vol. I, Bk. 1, Ch. 19*

150-151 At dawn the fishing boats are dragged into the water.

AFGHANISTAN

F OR CENTURIES BEFORE SEPTEM-
BER 11 AND OPERATION ENDURING
FREEDOM, AFGHANISTAN HAD BEEN
PLAGUED BY WARS, EARTHQUAKES,
FAMINE AND FLOODS, THOUGH THE REST
OF THE WORLD HEARD LITTLE ABOUT
THESE TRAVAILS.

In 1999, when I traveled there,
Afghanistan rarely made headlines and few
journalists were interested in traveling so
far to report on it. But we were there because
Marco Polo had crossed much of what is
now northern Afghanistan on his journey
out of Persia (modern Iran) toward China.

Though we knew that traveling through
Afghanistan's inhospitable terrain would be
tough, getting permission to enter the country at all was our first challenge. At that
time, the Taliban was in control of most of
Afghanistan, including the capital, Kabul,
while the Northern Alliance held onto the
North, the Panjshir Valley and the northern
territory west of Taloqan. That meant we
needed permission to travel from both war-
ring factions. The US office of the Taliban in

Flushing Meadows, Long Island informed us,
"You can come but not to photograph." No
need to go there.

Next we turned to the Northern
Alliance, also with offices in New York,
which represented the Afghan government
recognized by the United Nations and were
engaged in continual conflict with the
Taliban.

Things were not going well for the
Alliance. It was running out of money and
men, with only the great commander who
had beaten the Russians, Ahmad Shah Massoud, and troops loyal to him left to carry on
the fight from its base in the upper Panjshir
valley, so they welcomed us, eager for any
media exposure for their cause.

We then flew to London to meet Massoud's brother, Ahmad Mali Massoud, the
Afghan ambassador to Britain. He invited us
to travel to Afghanistan and showed us how
we could enter the country via Tajikstan. He
told us that that a military official would be
waiting at Dushanbe to escort us.

We got our visas and flew to Kazakhstan,

Jebal Saraj
A day with Massoud

153 Troops loyal to Ahmad Shah Massoud, leader of the Northern Alliance, aim th

idea of what we were getting into or where exactly we were going. The helicopter took off and flew just above tree level to evade the Taliban radar. As we approached the Panjshir valley, I was so engrossed in shooting the landscape just below us, trying to take advantage of the morning light, that I didn't stop to consider that flying with a pilot of unknown credentials in a battered Russian helicopter at low altitudes through a territory riddled with mines, with the possibility of being shot down by Pakistani jets working for the Taliban, was a fairly dangerous proposition. I just assumed, perhaps naively, that being under the protection of Massoud, who had defeated the Russians and was facing down the Taliban would be enough to keep us out of harm's way. I figured the Lion of Panjshir, and we, by association, were untouchable.

We knew Massoud loved the press. He was articulate, he loved literature, poetry

much more agile than our truck, and it quickly left us behind as we began to lumber up the mountains. A little farther up the road, we saw Massoud's vehicle halted at the top of a very steep hill. As we continued through the dust trying to catch up, we watched two ancient dilapidated tanks, captured from the Russians, also laboring up the steep slope.

We finally reached the top of the hill on foot, bathed in the brilliant light of sunset. A dozen or so men were straining to turn the turret of one of the tanks and turning the heavy cannon barrel to point directly west towards the sun that was about to disappear below the horizon.

Apart from Massoud and his men, I was alone up there; my interpreter and writer colleague, Mike Edwards, had remained behind, so I had no sure way of knowing exactly what was happening. I assumed the men were preparing for battle and started to take photographs non-stop. But then, at exactly 6:30, Massoud unwound the long scarf around his neck, spread it on the ground and knelt down in front of his tanks. With his men around him, they all began to pray. The light and the setting were ideal. It was the perfect photo op, almost too perfect. I wondered if this had all been set up for my benefit: the great leader piously asking Allah for strength in battle. There is no question that Massoud was a devout Muslim, but he was also devoted to seeking publicity for his cause. It occurred to me that this was Massoud's weakness: making himself available, and ultimately, vulnerable to the media. And so it was that two years later, on September 9, 2001, two Islamic terrorists claiming to be journalists ambushed and fatally wounded him during a phony interview. Even though he is gone, I will always see him on that day, the Lion of Panjshir, flanked by his soldiers and tanks, his face burning with the last rays of sun, facing Mecca in earnest prayer.

In retrospect, Afghanistan was by far the most fascinating stop on our itinerary. This is partly because the country is still so difficult to reach and because it was, before the 9/11 attack on New York's World Trade Center, a place that few photographers had ever visited.

But, even more dramatically, it is because the Afghanistan we visited was little changed from the territory that Marco Polo crossed in the thirteenth century. Afghanistan not only evokes the past, it exists in the past. Life in Afghanistan is just as difficult, crude and primitive as it was when Marco traveled there on his way to China. After twenty years of war and a peaceless period, Afghanistan has literally been bombed back to the Dark Ages. Just as in medieval times, in much of Afghanistan, and especially in the northern regions, there is no running water, no electricity, no telephones, and no cars (any that were available have been confiscated for military use). Donkeys are the main form of transportation. These conditions made the job of conveying the Afghanistan that Marco must have seen easy, but trying to make sense of the devastation left after two decades of war was impossible.

On one of our first nights in Afghanistan, traveling toward Feyzabad in the north, I experienced both this sense of exhilaration in seeing life as it must have been seven centuries ago and the shock of witnessing the far-ranging effects of war and violence on the Afghanis. Other than the headlights on our car, there was no other electric light.

We were approaching a city of a quarter-million people, and we could see nothing. All we could hear as we entered the city were shouts in the darkness and all we could see were boys — one just a child — as they appeared from the shadows with machine guns in their hands. They demanded to know who we were and what we were doing there. They allowed us to enter, and when we woke in the morning, we saw every man in the city was wearing the same kind of long tunics (*shalwarkameez*) that Afghans have worn for centuries. No one in northern Afghanistan wears clothes that seem to belong to our century. There are no logo t-shirts, no Nikes, no blue jeans. Today, as in Marco's time, they wear animal skins, tunics and turbans.

Marco ended up staying in Afghanistan longer than he had intended, as he fell ill and had to remain there with his party almost a year while he recuperated. He used the time well, studying Persian and Mongolian languages. It's not clear where he stayed, but it is believed to be near Badakhshan, on the edge of the Wakhan corridor. The Wakhan is a narrow strip of valley that runs between the Hindu Kush and Pakistan on the south side and the Pamir mountains and Tajikistan to the north. This sea of mountains made a big impression on Marco. He spoke of the high altitude and its effects on his body, adding that fire burned "not very hot."

On our trip there, we went to visit the local ruler of Wakhan, perhaps descended from the same line Marco met when he crossed the Corridor. The ruler invited us to his house where he was gathering his subjects for a sort of town meeting. Under pressure from the United Nations, he intended to announce a ban on the use of opium in his kingdom. The ruler was happy to have me record the event, and even asked me if I had ever seen opium being smoked. I replied that I hadn't, even though as a photographer working extensively in southeast Asia I had witnessed the ritual many times before. Before commanding the men of the village to hand over their pipes, he first ordered one man to lie down in front of me and smoke two pellets of the pitch-like substance, while I photographed the scene.

After Marco had recovered, he, his father and uncle and their companions resumed their journey east. With the year's delay, it would be a total of three years before they reached China. Once there, though, Marco would stay for 17 years.

AFGHANISTAN

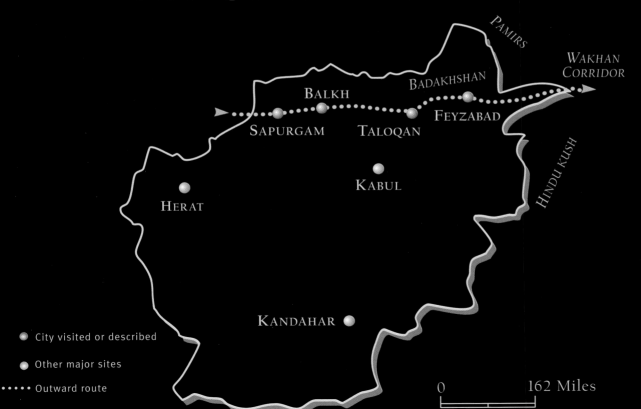

PAMIRS

WAKHAN
CORRIDOR

BADAKHSHAN

BALKH

FEYZABAD

SAPURGAM   TALOQAN

HINDU KUSH

KABUL

HERAT

KANDAHAR

● City visited or described

● Other major sites

•••• Outward route

0   162 Miles

Toward Panjshir

*"After leaving the town of Casem, you
ride for three days without finding a
single habitation, or anything to eat
or drink, so that you carry with you
everything that you require. "*

The Travels of Marco Polo, *Vol. I, Bk. 1, Ch. 28*

158-159 Flying toward the Panjshir valley
on a helicopter sent by Massoud.

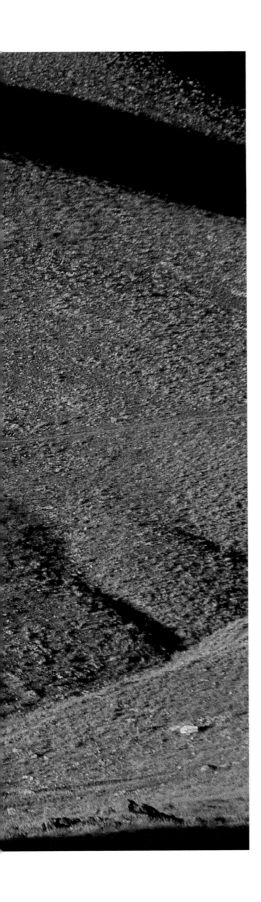

ALLIANCE OF THE NORTH
"TOMORROW WE FIGHT..."

160 A tank strains its way up the hill where Massoud is waiting.

161 An armed watch: the battle is near.

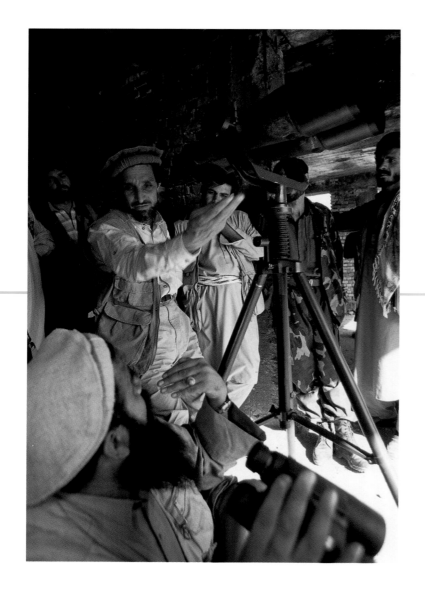

162 An enthusiastic lover of literature and poetry, Massoud was also a fine
strategist.

163 Massoud, the Lion of Panjshir, leads his officers in evening prayer.

War at the door

"You ride twelve days between east
and north-east, ascending a river that
runs through land belonging to a
brother of the Prince of Badakhshan.
[...] The people worship Mahommet,
and they have a peculiar language.
They are gallant soldiers."

The Travels of Marco Polo, *Vol. I, Bk. I, Ch. 32*

164-165 With his fellow-soldiers, an officer in
the Northern Alliance poses with his daughter.

The road to Badakhshan
Alexander's descendants

"Badakhshan [...] form a very great kingdom, and the royalty is hereditary. All those of the royal blood are descendent from King Alexander and the daughter of King Darius, who was Lord of the vast Empire of Persia."

The Travels of Marco Polo, *Vol. I, Bk. 1, Ch. 29*

166-167 A river valley near Taloqan.

TALOQAN
A LAND OF SHEPHERDS AND WARRIORS

168-169 A group of proud inhabitants in the
province of Takhar advance on Taloqan.

"They all wear drawers made of cotton cloth, and into the making of these some will put 60, 80, or even 100 ells of stuff. This they do to make themselves look large in the hips, for the men of those parts think that to be a great beauty in a woman."

The Travels of Marco Polo, *Vol. I, Bk. 1, Ch. 29*

TALOQAN
THE WHEAT MARKET

170 and 171 Women in traditional costumes heading for the Taloqan market, known as Taican by Marco Polo.

Baharak

172 Rows of Russian armored vehicles rust in the streets and fields of Afghanistan.

173 Completely veiled by her burkha, a woman takes her children to a doctor in Feyzabad.

"Sweeter than honey..."

"It has great plenty of everything, but especially of the very best melons in the world. They preserve them by paring them round and round into strips, and drying them in the sun. When dry they are sweeter than honey."

The Travels of Marco Polo, *Vol. I, Bk. 1, Ch. 26*

174-175 A watermelon-seller takes his goods to Taloqan market.

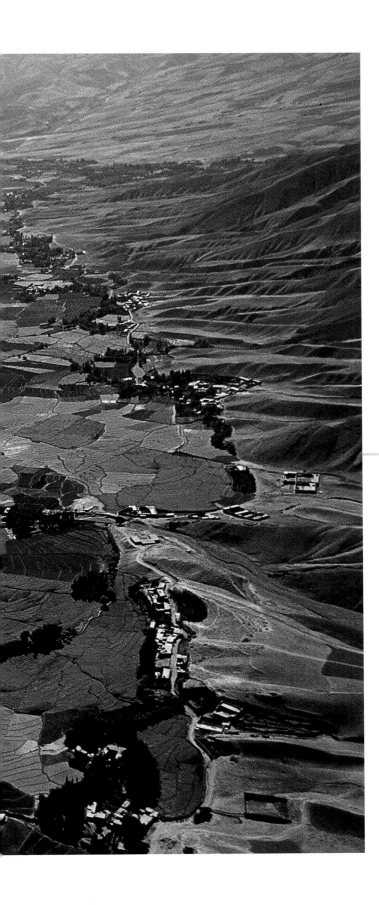

FLYING TO FEYZABAD

*"Those mountains are so lofty that 'tis a
hard day's work, from morning till
evening, to get to the top of them. On
getting up, you find an extensive plain,
with great abundance of grass and trees,
and copious springs of pure water
running down through rocks and ravines."*

The Travels of Marco Polo, *Vol. I, Bk. 1, Ch. 29*

176-177 In the area of Feyzabad, fields stretch as
far as the eye can see.

FEYZABAD
THE ENDLESS FLOCK

"In the mountains there are vast numbers of sheep—400, 500, or 600 in a single flock, and all of them wild; and though many of them are taken, they never seem to get aught the scarcer."

The Travels of Marco Polo, *Vol. I, Bk. 1, Ch. 29*

178-179 Still plentiful, sheep are one of Feyzabad's few local resources.

180-181 A new dawn in Feyzabad awakening from the darkness brought by years of war.

FEYZABAD
THE MARKETPLACE

182 and 183 In Feyzabad, like in every other bazaar in the Middle East, basic goods make a colorful display in the bazaar.

Feyzabad
The city of salt

184 Weighing blocks of salt in Feyzabad market.

185 Day laborers waiting to be offered work.

CARAVANSERAI
THE INNS OF ISLAM

"They wear nothing on the head but a cord some ten palms long twisted round it."

The Travels of Marco Polo, *Vol. I, Bk. 1, Ch. 28*

186-187 Mules are loaded with salt in the courtyard of a *caravanserai* in Feyzabad.

"Good wheat is grown, and also barley without husk. They have no olive oil, but make oil from sesame, and also from walnuts."

The Travels of Marco Polo, *Vol. I, Bk. 1, Ch. 29*

188-189 Separating the seed from the chaff in Badakhshan.

Feyzabad
A bread oven

190-191 Making bread the traditional way.
The ingredients are excellent wheat flour, good
quality salt and pure water.

The Pamirs
The roof of the world

192-193 Horses graze freely in the meadows of the foothills.

194-195 Glaciers and thin air on the roof of the world: This is the Pamir plateau.

The Wakhan Corridor
On the Way to China

"There are numbers of wild bests of all sorts in this region. And when you leave this little country, and ride three days north-east, always among mountains, you get to such a height that 'tis said to be highest place in the world!"

The Travels of Marco Polo, *Vol. I, Bk. 1, Ch. 32*

196-197 Heading east along the bed of a dried-up river.

"The people worship Mahommet, and they have a peculiar language. They are gallant soldiers, and they have a chief whom they call NONE, which is as much as to say Count."

The Travels of Marco Polo, *Vol. I, Bk. 1, Ch. 32*

198 and 199 The Shah of Wakhan, said Ismail, greets his subjects with a traditional salute.

WAHKAN
IN THE BARE HEART OF ASIA

200-201 A child sleeps in a hammock.
Little has changed since the thirteenth century.

Wahkan
Ageless children

202 left A group of children display the skull of an *Ovis poli* (Polo's sheep).

02 right and 203 Education in the Wakhan orridor is provided by tradition and nature.

204-205 The Corridor comes to an end: China is just over the horizon.

MARCO POLO
in CHINA

INTRODUCTION

Coming down from high altitudes is more dangerous than climbing.

The paths that wind between the rocks and along the edges of bottomless ravines are narrow, icy and slippery. The line of camels gets tangled and the creatures lose their balance, the loads slip and then risk falling into the abyss that the mist renders unfathomable. Furthermore, the camel-drivers put their own lives at risk as they do their best to save their animals and goods.

The descent represented more than a month of slipping on stones and fording torrents, all the while spied upon by mountain-dwellers squatting on peaks like hairy beasts, 'idolaters, wild and wicked.' Forty days were required in all until they reached the plateau where Kashgar lies. Kashgar was a longed-for destination by all those who followed the ancient Silk Road, a city of tens of thousands of inhabitants that seemed a metropolis to the exhausted travelers after the desert of bare and uninhabited mountains. They were cheered by the sight of gardens, orchards, vineyards and cotton fields. But Marco restrained their enthusiasm and noted that the merchants in Kashgar seemed stingy and miserable 'because they drink and eat poorly.' Who knows what they had prepared for the poor survivors of the Pamir plateau to make him so cynical.

Once they had got their strength back, they set off once more to Yarkand where they found the citizens suffering from goiters because of the deficiencies in the water they drank. From there to Hotan and its cotton fields, and Peym where the river waters carry jasper and chalcedony, and where a strange custom is practiced: when a man has to stay away for more than three weeks, his wife immediately remarries and he too can take another wife. From there the three went to Cherchen that lay in the midst of sands and brackish water; though an inhospitable environment, these features protected the town because when the inhabitants saw an enemy band, they left Cherchen en masse and hid in the sandy plains close to some water source. As the wind blows non-stop in that region, their footprints in the sand were hidden; the enemies could not find them and would have to leave humiliated.

These are all desolate, bare regions, but the desert proper begins after the city of Lop, which stands on the threshold of the Gobi like the shore overlooking a dry sea. Here the Polos rested for at least a week to gather their strength before tackling the desert. This empty expanse is so large that anyone wishing to cross its widest section would take at least a year, but the caravan route cuts it where there is a sort of isthmus that reduces the miserable experience to little more than a month. There are of course no living creatures of any sort because there is no water and therefore no vegetation, however, the Gobi Desert is filled with spirits and nocturnal and diurnal ghosts that deceive and lead the lone traveler astray. If you sleep apart from a main group at night, it will sound as

209 left Funeral in the kingdom of Tangut: the burning coffin is at the center of a joyous celebration.

209 right In his park at Chengdu, Kublai hunts deers, hinds and wild boars with a saker falcon.

209

though your companions are calling you, and if you head towards their calls, you will lose the caravan and never find it again. By day, if you are left behind your companions, you may think you are following the right direction to catch up with them but it is an illusion that will take you to your death: so never, ever leave the group even when you hear the sound of trumpets and drums above you as though an army were passing overhead.

No specter succeeded in leading Marco and his relations astray and they finally emerged on the other side of the ocean of sand after a thirty-day march. They arrived in the province of Tangut, a land of idolaters and Buddhist monasteries, where the inhabitants would sacrifice rams at the foot of statues for the benefit of their health and the pros-

perity of their children. They would give part of the animals to the priests, eat the rest and keep the bones in decorated caskets. Marco was struck by their funerary ceremonies: here the bodies were cremated with paper figures in the form of men, horses, camels and coins, and the more that were burned, the richer the deceased would be in the hereafter.

But the custom that struck the Venetians most was found in the nearby province of Kamul where the rules of hospitality are taken so far that when a traveler enters a house, not only is he given food to eat and a place to sleep, the husband will also go away for a few days and leave his guest his wife. They do this because they believe that their generosity will bring them good crops and fodder.

210 A human guinea-pig offers the Khan a demonstration of the virtues of asbestos.

They followed the Iguristan, whose first king was not born of a woman but a plant; then the Sain-Taras where the people made clothes from asbestos and, when the clothes got dirty, they did not wash them in water but put them on the fire so that they turned white again. This material was what Europeans call salamander, which is not a creature but a mineral. Rhubarb grows near the Su-Ciu but there is also a poisonous grass that will make the hooves of the livestock that it eat fall off. In the city of Kan-ciu there were idols made of gold and the men there had up to thirty wives each.

And finally, right at the other end of Asia, the city of Kaipingfu (Xanadu) appeared, which was not a city at all but the summer residence of the Great Khan. It was the reserve he maintained for the Mongols' greatest passion, hunting. It was an immense expanse of land enclosed by a wall sixteen miles round, enclosing woods, rivers and meadows and deer of all kinds.

Kublai loved hawking (he had two hundred, all perfectly trained) and also hunting with a tame leopard that would leap from his saddle to attack its prey. In the middle of this enclosure there was a large marble palace with gilded rooms but, mindful of the tents of his nomadic forefathers, the emperor preferred to live in a mobile palace made from bamboo, also sculpted, decorated and gilded, and supported by two hundred cords of silk. The roof was made purely of bamboo but so skillfully that not a single drop of water could enter; however, it never rained because Kublai kept Tibetan wizards and sorcerers in his service who were so expert in the arts of enchantment that when bad weather arrived, they ensured the clouds did not pass over the palace. Rain might fall all around but not on the palace.

This was the setting for the Great Khan's audience with the three Venetians a few days after their arrival. He was happy to see them again and politely passed

211 left The Polo brothers, already known to the Great Khan, introduce young Marco to Kublai's court.

211 right A pair of greyhounds follow a deer in Kublai's park at Khanbaliq (Beijing).

over the absence of the one hundred wise men. He was cheered at receiving the oil from the Church of the Holy Sepulcher that would make his mother happy, and he asked who the young man was that accompanied his two old acquaintances. Nicolò proudly presented his son, who clearly made a good impression on Kublai, and the Khan immediately took Marco into his own retinue though without a precise function. Marco learnt the customs of the Mongols, the imperial rites and ceremonies and perfected his mastery of the many languages spoken by the subjects of one of the largest states the world had ever known. The intelligent and quick-witted Marco was ready to make himself useful when the occasion presented itself.

A bond of enduring affection and friendship sprang up between the Khan, in his sixties, and the twenty-year-old apprentice courtier. Kublai liked to surround himself with men from far-flung countries, he appreciated the diversity of their cultures and mentalities and knew how best to exploit them to govern his empire.

The Venetian trio therefore followed the itinerant court on its travels. Toward the end of August, the Great Khan left Kaipingfu and moved to the Mongolian steppes for a sacred ceremony.

In this land where ten thousand snow-white horses were bred, the Khan had to sprinkle a little of their milk in the air and on the ground so that Heaven would protect all that belonged to him: men, women, animals, birds, cities and land. And no-one could drink of this milk except the descendants of Genghis Khan and the members of a Mongol tribe whose ancestors once saved the life of the great conqueror.

After this ritual had been performed, it was time to return to the capital of Cathay. This was the emperor's winter residence and thus named Khanbaliq, 'the abode of the Khan', and which today we call Beijing. To the Venetians, Khanbaliq was enormous: their home, Venice, was at the time, after Naples and Paris, the third largest city in Europe with 100,000 inhabitants; Khanbaliq, however, was twelve times larger with 1,200,000 inhabitants according to a census taken a few years earlier, in 1270. Here Marco first came into contact with the astronomical numbers that were to make him famous. In addition to the teeming inhabitants in the endless criss-cross of streets and alleys, there were merchants who converged here from every region of Cathay and even India, bringing costly goods like gold, gems, silver, spices and pearls. More than a thousand carts a day entered the city bringing silk alone. And all these

precious goods were paid, not in ready cash like in Europe, but with small notes of paper made from mulberry bark on which were printed various red symbols denoting their value. Everyone accepted these notes and trusted them because they were guaranteed by the Great Khan, and anyone who dared to produce counterfeit versions was condemned to die an atrocious death.

There were few wrong-doers in Khanbaliq, which was the safest city in the world; it had one thousand guards for each of its twelve gates and was continuously patrolled by soldiers on horseback. When darkness fell, a great bell would chime and after the third stroke, everyone had to be indoors. Only doctors and midwives were allowed to tour the city at night. The instigators of this surveillance were the court astrologers who had advised the Great Khan not to trust his Chinese subjects. Kublai believed their forecasts and rewarded them with gifts, food and clothing, and the astrologers prospered making predictions of disasters and happiness. In the capital alone there were more than five thousand.

It was the astrologers that suggested to the Great Khan that he should build a separate city, close to Khanbaliq, enclosed by a triple ring of walls in the center of which, surrounded by a large park of domestic and wild animals, should stand the imperial palace. This alone covered a square mile with its marble buildings and ceramic roofs painted shades of red, yellow, green and blue. The rooms were adorned with sculpted and gilded dragons, paintings of battles, and statues

212 top
Presentation of two chests containing paper money before the Great Khan.

212 bottom
Following the hunt at the end of May, the Khan proclaims three days of festivities

213 Kublai celebrates the anniversary of the kingdom with his four wives and two officials.

of warriors, birds and wild animals. In one of the gardens stood a manmade hill one hundred feet high planted with superb trees because as soon as Kublai heard of a fine tree, wherever it was, he would have it dug up and carried by elephant to his park. He also had a stable of ten thousand horses, all as white as milk. He had thousands of concubines that nearly all came from a province of Mongolia called Ungut, which was renowned for the beauty of its women. Every two years, imperial officials would scour the district to choose four or five hundred girls. The Great Khan had only four wives, all of whom bore the title of empress and had a personal court of no fewer than ten thousand pages and ladies-in-waiting.

The festivities held in the enclosure of the impe-

rial palace astounded Marco, for example, those held on the Khan's birthday, 28 September. On this day, Kublai had everything draped with gold cloth, a material that he and ten thousand 'barons and knights' wore. He received gifts from every part of the empire and 'all the Tartars of the world' celebrated lavishly. No less important were the New Year festivities that fell in February. On this occasion Kublai and all his people dressed in white – the color of good omen – and gifts of all kinds would arrive, though preferably white. Each province sent him hundreds of white horses, making a total of ten thousand, and five thousand elephants covered with silk caparisons and bearing caskets of gold and silver tableware to be used at the New Year banquet. Everyone paraded before the Khan and there were

214 left Pulisangin bridge near Khanbaliq could be crossed by ten horsemen abreast.

214 right Quinsay, today Hangzhou, impressed Marco by its size and 12,000 bridges.

215 The Khan is presented with pearls and precious stones from Yunnan, which were his exclusive property.

so many that the procession lasted hours. Those who could not enter due to the throng were obliged to remain outside but the Great Khan looked on them just the same from the walls of the palace and they paid tribute to him by prostrating themselves before him.

These were the functionaries and 'barons' who had come from provinces near and far, some of whom had traveled for months to arrive in time. The journey, however, was a safe one as the Pax Mongolica stretched right across the empire, as far as Korea and Persia. Like in ancient Rome, many roads led from Khanbaliq across the vast territories, each one named after the province it led to ('which is very wise', commented Marco). On each of these roads there was a posting station every twenty five miles where horses could be changed and food and accommodation were provided.

Travelers, messengers and envoys could therefore travel comfortably across the massive distances that separated the capital from the frontiers.

These were the roads that Marco took when he became one of Kublai's trusted officials. He traveled far and wide through Cathay and Mangi (as *Il Milione* refers to the two Chinas, the northern section conquered by Genghis Khan a half century earlier, and the southern one that Kublai was occupying). While Marco's father and uncle toured the empire, enriching themselves with commerce and accumulating a large quantity of jewels to take back to Venice, Marco was visiting the remotest provinces on missions for the Khan, and accumulating information for his master and future readers of *Il Milione*. His enthusiasm was fired by a city named Quinsai (the capital of southern China that is today named Hangzhou) which was an Asiatic equivalent of Venice.

It lies around a maze of canals and bridges (twelve thousand), the tallest of which allow the largest transport junks to pass below. Its ten markets contained everything under the sun, including deer, ducks and sea, lake and river fish. But the local pride was its courtesans who, from Marco's description, seem the most fascinating in the world because 'foreigners who disport themselves with them once are left beside themselves, and are so won over by their gentleness and charms that they can never forget them; and once they return home they tell that they have been to Quinsai – the City of Heaven – and do nothing but look forward to their return.'

In the company of an old gentleman who had lived at the court of the last Sung emperor before the Mongol conquest, Marco went to visit the Sung imperial palace, which was no more than a pitiful ruin of past greatness, an architectural marvel abandoned, where now lizards and brambles proliferated. Having passed through the high perimeter walls ten miles long, Marco admired the huge pavilions, gold and blue columns, and walls frescoed with the histories of ancient rulers. Every year, the old courtier remembered nostalgically, the emperor held a banquet here to which not only dignitaries were invited, but also craftsmen and merchants, up to ten thousand people (after one million, ten thousand is the figure that most often appears in Marco's description of China). And in the park, 'he went to entertain himself with his damsels, some in carts, some on horseback, and no man entered there.' When they were tired of hunting, the girls undressed in the woods and bathed naked in the pools while the emperor watched them with 'very great pleasure.'

One at a time, during the years of his long stay in China, Marco visited the less accessible regions, places that his imperial colleagues only knew by hearsay. On his every return to Khanbaliq, he delighted Kublai with his accounts, just as he still enchants us today. The desert highlands of Tibet were populated by lions and other wild beasts, and were so extensive that it took twenty days to cross them. When travelers camped for the night, they frightened away the beasts by creating large fires with the canes that grew there to an enormous height. The Tibetans were also the most knowledgeable necromancers in the world, able to create great storms of lightning and thunder.

In the nearby province of Gansu (the Tibetan Kham), there was a salt-water lake where pearls were fished, and on the hills enormous herds of musk deer wandered whose smell was evident for miles around. In Sichuan, the city of Chengdu was divided by a river so wide that it seemed like a sea, but, nonetheless, a long and wide stone bridge had been built across it with enough marble columns to support a roof, between which the wooden boxes of the merchants were laid out each morning and taken away each evening.

The province of Yunnan was infested by crocodiles and serpents able to swallow a man entire, but even more dangerous than these were the inhabitants because they would kill anyone who proved to be their superior physically or intellectually; their reasoning being that the souls of those killed remained in their houses and protected them with their virtues.

In the province of Jiangsu the men and women covered their teeth with thin plaques of gold and tattooed their arms and legs. When a baby was born, the father would take to his bed and remain there for fifty days, receiving the congratulations of family and friends as though it was he who had given birth. Kublai listened, laughed and was amazed at these stories, then he sent his special envoy off on another mission to learn more extraordinary facts.

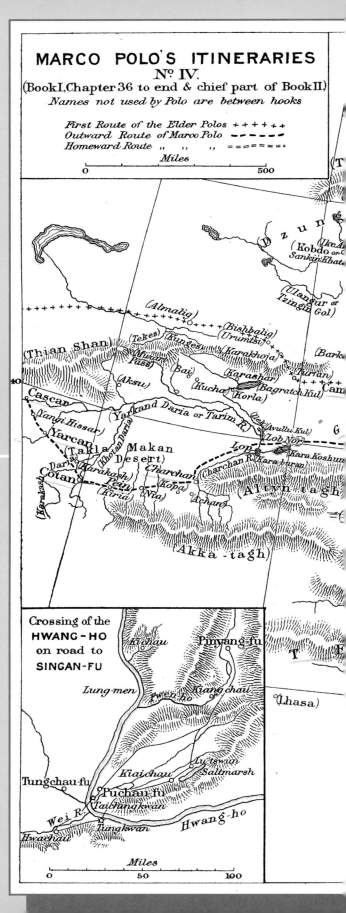

IN THE LAND
OF THE KHAN

SIR HENRY YULE'S SECOND GENERAL map shows the differences between the trip made by the Polo brothers alone — who crossed Asia much further north, beyond the Tian Shan mountain range — and the journey undertaken with Marco through the Taklimakan Desert and Turfan Depression.

PLAN OF SHANGTU
From an Eye-Sketch by Dr S.W.Bushell,1872

Kublai's Park

Earthen Wall

City Wall

PALACE
Wall

0   1   2 Miles
Deduced Approx Scale

River Shangtu
(Lower down Lan-ho)

MICHAEL YAMASHITA

CHINA
FROM THE PAMIRS TO KASHGAR

WITH THE PAMIR MOUNTAINS LOOMING ABOVE THEM, THE WAKHAN AND KILIK PASSES LEAD INTO THE FLAT IMMENSITY OF CENTRAL ASIA AT ALMOST 16,250 FEET, LIKE GASHES IN A GIGANTIC FORTRESS.

This is the logical point to enter China from Afghanistan, and it is the route Marco Polo took. But today, the border between the two countries is closed, which meant that with the overland route blocked, we had to fly back from Feyzabad to Dushanbe in Tajikistan, before flying on to China. And then there was the minor problem of what to fly in, as Taloqan, where Massoud's emissaries had dropped us off, had since been taken by the Taliban, and there were no other helicopters available to get us out of Afghanistan. We wound up hitching a ride with a United Nations transport plane dropping supplies in Feyzabad on its way to Dushanbe. Because it was already loaded, we had to board with only the clothes we were wearing (and cameras), leaving the rest of our bags and camping equipment on the tarmac. Once we made it to Dushanbe, we flew on to Beijing. From there, we had to backtrack about 2600 miles and fly to Kashgar in Xinjiang, China's westernmost province. We drove to Taxkorgan along the Karakorum Highway, on the western edge of the Taklimakan Desert. After all that, we wound up just a few dozen miles from where we'd left off in Afghanistan, at the Wakhan Corridor leading out of the Pamirs.

Getting a visa to enter China, especially as a journalist, is just as complicated. China does not offer the luxury of choosing when to visit. Nor does it allow journalists to travel freely throughout the country. The provincial authorities in this remote area near the Pamirs are especially sensitive about members of the press traveling there, as they would prefer not to publicize the presence of rebel groups in the region. Various separatist movements used to train in Taliban camps in Afghanistan, as we now know since September 11, 2001. Special permission must be granted to travel in this region.

We had hoped to visit in the spring, when even the desert blooms with color, and the grasslands are dotted with breathtaking wild flowers. The authorities replied that they were too busy to worry about us in the spring. The best they could do was March, not the best time to work in this area. The last of winter lingers well into March here, and the desert then is a monotonous expanse — no snow, no color, just unending shades of brown — but we had no choice. As photographer's luck would have it, though, that year there were some unexpected snow storms in mid-March. They were not heavy but enough to sprinkle the vast plains and distant mountains with a white dust. And in the middle of the desert, we encountered a blizzard. One of our goals on this trip was to show the hazardships of travel in Marco Polo's time, and the weather cooperated nicely.

THE PAMIR PLATEAU
XINJIANG

ROM THE PAMIRS TO KASHGAR

PAMIR PLATEAU

GOBI DESERT

INNER MONGOLIA

XINJIANG

TANGUT

Yellow River

BEIJING

KASHGAR
YARKAND

QINGHAI

HOTAN

JIANGSU

SHANGHAI

TIBET

SICHUAN

Yangtze River

● City visited or described

● Other major sites

YUNNAN

HONG KONG

From our base in Taxkorgan, we set out to explore the area. Though we rarely veered from Marco's itinerary, along the way there were some unexpected, but welcome surprises that he had not mentioned. One was the village of Tiznot, a village where all the females, from infancy to old age, wear only red clothing. The males are free to choose any color but they avoid red. They, like Massoud and many Afghans, are Tajik, one of the major tribes of the Pamir area. They found themselves suddenly Chinese when the Communists took over in 1949. The Chinese closed the border so that these people, who were Afghans, were now confined to the territory of the newly-born People's Republic. Though their ability to move back and forth over the borders they once crossed freely is restricted, life for the Tajiks here is vastly different from that of their brothers and sisters on the other side in Afghanistan. It was heartening to see these "ladies in red" whose beautiful eyes and faces were set off by the ruby brilliance of their clothes. It was a huge contrast from the somber blues and grays of the burkhas worn by Afghan women, whose faces I almost never saw. Cheering, too, was the sight of children playing in a school yard at recess. Schools were nonexistent where I had just been on the other side of the border. Filled with color, smiles and laughter, this village was a photographer's dream.

In this area, minorities, including the Tajiks, Kazakhs, Kyrgyz (pronounced Keer-geez) and Mongols, actually outnumber the Han people, the majority population of China. And outnumbering all the other minorities, as well as the Han, are Muslim Uighurs (pronounced Wee-gurs), whom Marco Polo wrote about. Marco described in detail the beliefs of each of the many groups he encountered here: the worshippers of Mohammed, Nestorian Christians and those he referred to as "adorers of idols," i.e., Buddhists.

In addition to describing the local people in detail, Marco was also struck by the vast market in Kashgar which, was one of the largest in the world in the thirteenth century. Today it is still the biggest market in central Asia, and arguably the world. Once again, I was struck by the contrast between life here on the Chinese side of the Pamirs and that in Afghanistan. At Kashgar, you can find almost any product imaginable; in Afghanistan, especially in the north where we had just been, practically nothing. Every Sunday thousands of people converge on Kashgar from the countryside to sell their goods — from produce, to livestock, to noodles, strands and strands of noodles made from a wide variety of grains, including rice, soya and wheat. Kashgar is said to produce the best noodles in China.

The question of noodles is a matter of some debate among Marco Polo scholars and aficionados. Did Marco Polo bring this type of stringy pasta back to Venice from China? Or was it the other way around? Marco talks little about himself, much less food, in his book, and not once does he refer to what we call pasta. Some say pasta could be found in Italy before Marco made his journey, and so was not a novelty for him. It's not certain when it was first imported, but it's most likely that it was brought by Arab merchants. I never found an answer to this question, but I did enjoy the research. The local specialty, lamien, is one of my favorite dishes, and I photographed every bowl I ate — at breakfast, lunch and dinner.

222-223 Rare spring snowfall in the Pamirs on the edge of the Taklimakan desert.

KARAKULI LAKE
LOST WATERS

"And when you have got to this height you find a great lake between two mountains, and out of it a fine river running through a plain clothed with the finest pasture in the world; insomuch that a lean beast there will fatten to your heart's content in ten days."

The Travels of Marco Polo, *Vol. I, Bk. 1, Ch. 32*

224-225 Karakuli is in one of the remotest sections of the Pamirs.

THE ROAD TO KASHGAR

226 Road accidents are a common sight on this stretch of the Silk Road.

"*Their houses are circular, and are made of wands covered with felts. There are carried along with them whithersoever they go; for the wands are so strongly bound together, and likewise so well combined, that the frame can be made very light.*"

The Travels of Marco Polo, *Vol. I, Bk. 1, Ch. 52*

228-229 Baking naan (bread) inside a yurt in Datar, a village in the Chinese section of the Pamirs.

THE CHINESE PAMIRS
THE PILLARS OF THE SKY

"The people dwell high up in the mountains, are savage idolaters, living only by the chase, and clothing themselves in the skin of beasts. In truth an evil race."

The Travels of Marco Polo, *Vol. I, Bk. 1, Ch. 32*

230-231 A young Tajik leads her donkey through the immensity of the Chinese Pamirs.

Tajik land
The water of life

232 Tajik girls from Akmiqit go to collect water.

233 The precious liquid is collected from a pool in an oasis.

School in Tiznot
Color Code

234 Tajik children wait for their lessons to start.

235 In this corner of the world females, following
traditions, wear red while males wear blue.

FUTURE GROVES
POPLAR PLANTATIONS

236-237 The only trees in
the Hotan region are
grown in rows.

TOWARD KASHGAR
THE ASIAN MARKET

*"Cascar is a region lying between
north-east and east, and constituted a
kingdom in former days, but now it is
subject to the Great Khan. The people
worship Mahommet."*

The Travels of Marco Polo, *Vol. I, Bk. I, Ch. 33*

238-239 A snow storm near Kashgar, the biggest
city between the Pamirs and Taklimakan.

240-241 Every Sunday, thousands of people
converge on Kashgar for the market.

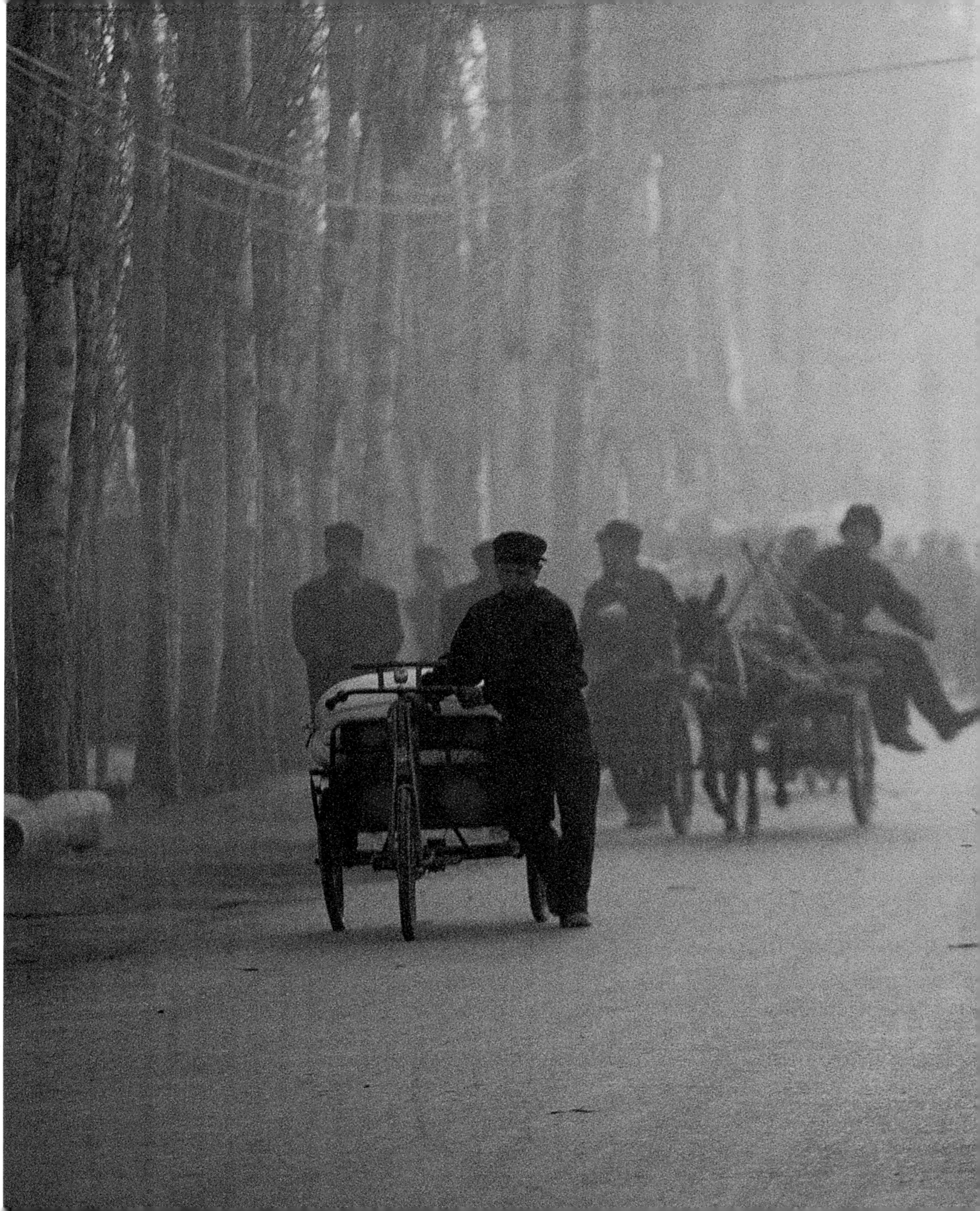

KASHGAR

"*There are a good number of towns and villages, but the greatest and finest is Cascar itself. Inhabitants live by trade and handicrafts. [...] From this country many merchants go forth about the world on trading journeys.*"

The Travels of Marco Polo, *Vol. I, Bk. 1, Ch. 33*

242-243 As the hours pass, the market gets busier.

244 The market in Kashgar is not just buying and selling: the billiard tables are a center of attraction

ETHNIC CROSSROADS

245 Business is done between people from many and very different ethnic groups.

Kashgar

The Western Frontier

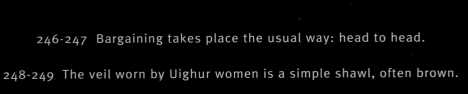

246-247 Bargaining takes place the usual way: head to head.

248-249 The veil worn by Uighur women is a simple shawl, often brown.

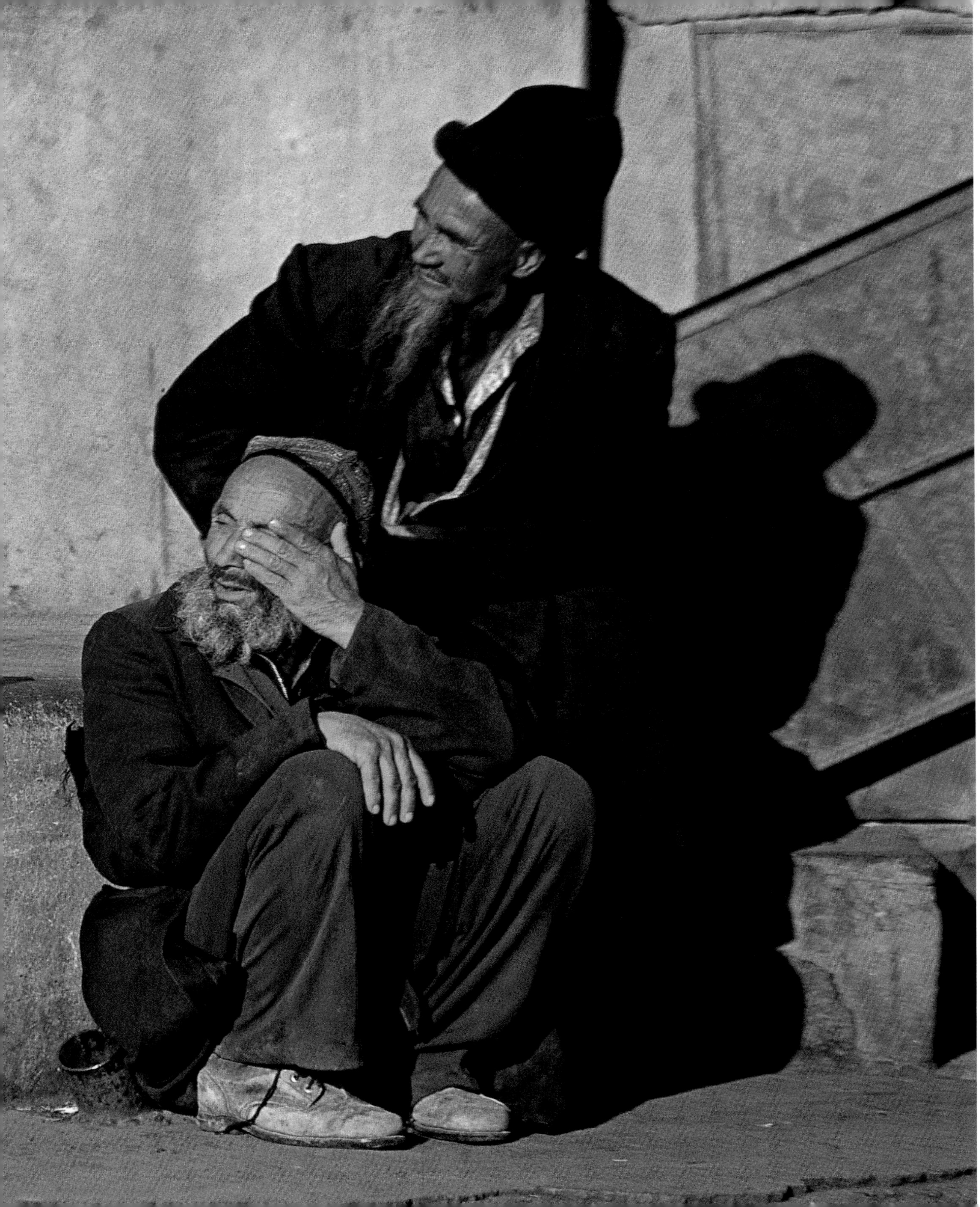

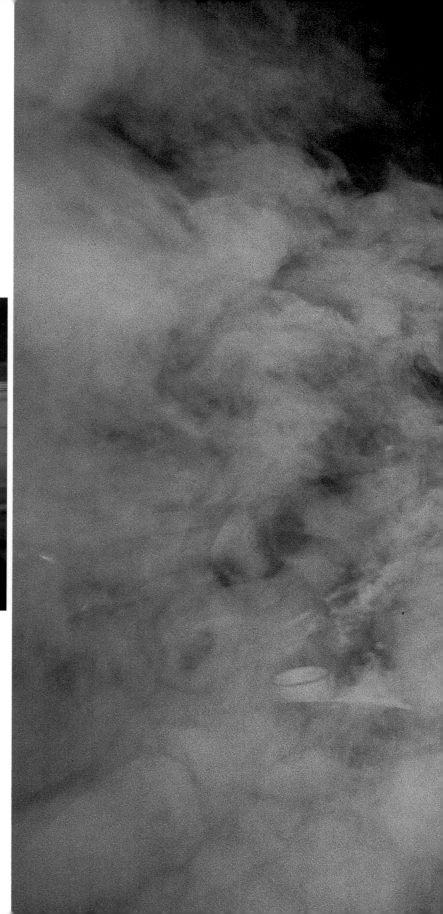

CHINESE SPAGHETTI
DID MARCO BRING IT TO CHINA?

250 and 251 Tiao zi, literally 'pulled strings,'
are made only by hand.

252-253 Noodles in Kashgar are considered
the best in China.

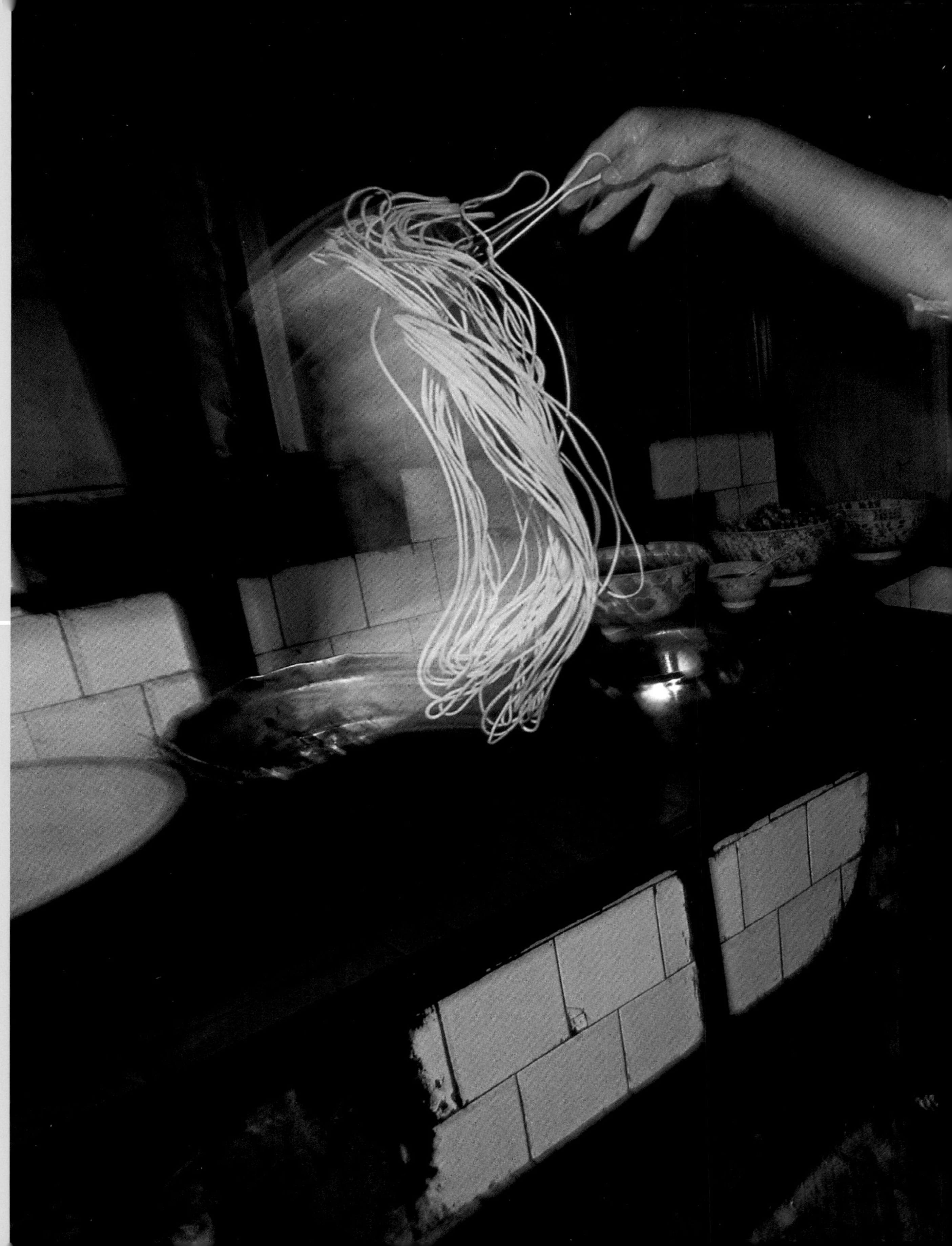

MICHAEL YAMASHITA

CHINA
FROM KASHGAR TO XANADU

IN A VILLAGE NOT FAR FROM HOTAN, ON THE SOUTHERN BOUNDARY OF THE TAKLIMAKAN DESERT, MESSER POLO ENCOUNTERED A RATHER UNUSUAL LOCAL CUSTOM EN ROUTE TO KUBLAI KHAN'S XANADU.

When a visitor arrived in the town, he would be invited home by one of the local men and asked to choose from all the women in the household, wives or daughters included. The visitor was free to entertain himself with her in any manner and for as long as he liked. In the meantime, the husband made himself scarce.

We found no trace of this unusually hospitable place, though we tried very hard to locate it. Chinese scholars have confirmed that the practice of sharing wives and daughters with foreign visitors was indeed an ancient tradition in remote areas, the theory being that it helped widen the gene pool, avoiding the threat of marriages between blood relations. Marco, who was an impressionable 17 when he passed through here,

elaborates on the charms of the local populace, especially the women, and from what we saw and photographed, their descendants share equally beautiful attributes.

Although we missed visiting the fabled village, we did find the cotton cultivation described by Marco. In one of the fields I photographed, I watched a young woman with a crutch as she bent over to plant seeds under the plastic ground cover that protected against excessive evaporation. The solitary planter, with just one leg, made her way slowly across the 300-foot field, supported only by the crutch as she crouched to put the seeds in the ground.

But a more important commodity than cotton was the production of the fiber that gave the Silk route its name. Today most of the silk exported from China is made in factories, but we were looking for traditional techniques used during Marco's time. We found what we were looking for in the villages around Hotan in the Xinjiang desert where silk is still produced by hand. Just as in

JIAYUGUAN
THE SENTINEL IN THE DESERT

255 Jiayuguan fort stands at the western end of the Great Wall.

260-261 Young Uighurs in Hotan. Polo noted the physical beauty of this people.

the thirteenth century, women boil silkworm cocoons in large pots placed on concrete ovens in the floor. The resulting fibers are then spun into threads on large spindles the size of a bicycle wheel, dyed, and then woven on hand and foot driven looms.

Having been transported back to Marco's time once again, we aimed for another one of Marco's destinations. Marco was the first Westerner to comment on the "sands that sing" a mournful wail produced by the wind blowing across the towering (up to 1000 feet high) sand dunes of the Taklimakan desert around Dunhuang, prompting many to consider the area haunted by spirits. Today it's hard to hear much of anything besides the noise of crowds, as it's one of the region's most popular tourist attractions, especially for Chinese travelers. I was disappointed by all the activity, though this spot was probably just as busy during Marco's time. But the question was how to get a picture that said thirteenth century without the twenty-first century crowds. I tried walking to the other side of a huge dune, away from the crowds. A line of camels about to pass by seemed like the perfect opportunity for a graphic frame. However, as they approached, I could see that

each camel was wearing an identification number, like ponies for hire at a carnival ride, spoiling the illusion. But the light was right, so I went ahead and shot the desert procession back lit, under-exposed (obscuring the numbers in shadows), and silhouetted against the massive white dune.

Marco also speaks of the temples of a long-established Buddhist sect in Dunhuang, notable because they are carved out of the mountainside, and now known as the Mogao Caves. What he doesn't mention is that inside the caves are some of the most important and ancient Buddhist artworks in the world. Around the fifth century AD, the caves in Mogao began to attract a community of Buddhist monks that flourished rapidly in this oasis in the desert. Over six centuries, the monks decorated the caves with religious paintings with a wide variety of themes, from representations of the life of Buddha to more mundane scenes. One, in particular, impressed me, as it was so suited to our story: against a typical Chinese landscape, bandits armed with swords fall on a group of travelers, perhaps merchants like Marco. Raids by bandits were a constant threat to merchant caravans, as they crossed long stretches of deserted desert with their wares. Although it is possible to shoot pictures in the caves, it can be an expensive proposition. The curators of the temples charge photographers $150 per square meter of mural. Though I am not accustomed to paying for pictures, in this case, the uncanny depiction of scenes that could have illustrated Marco's book warranted an exception.

After I selected the sections of the murals that interested me most, a clerk followed me, calculator in hand, to measure them. I had to choose very carefully, as a single photograph could cost over $2000. Not only was the choice expensive, it also came with strings attached. There were restrictions on how to light the artworks. No hot lights were allowed, and as I was not carrying a large enough strobe to light one of the large-scale murals in the pitch black of the caves, I had to be inventive. We solved the problem by taking the mirrors off the walls of our hotel rooms and using them to bounce light from the sun into the cave, bending it on a second angle and then using a diffuser to finally bathe the subject in soft sunlight.

Though his account was dazzling to his contemporaries, Marco showed surprising restraint in describing many of his experiences. For example, he matter-of-factly describes a statue of a reclining Buddha in Zhangye, where he supposedly spent a year. When I went to photograph the site, I was surprised to see that Marco had neglected to mention that this particular statue is actually over 100 feet in length, and is the largest reclining Buddha in the world. My widest wide-angle lens was barely big enough to fit the Buddha inside a 35-mm frame.

His book was also a catalog of commodities. In addition to reporting on Persian oil, Marco was also the first to describe asbestos, fireproof fibers mined in China to produce what he called "material that does not burn." He also described a "rock that burns" — coal, which was almost unknown in Europe at the time. When we asked to visit the asbestos mine a few miles south of us in Gansu, the largest one of its kind in China, we were turned down, but we were allowed to photograph the processing of the stone cotton, as the fiber is called. To a Westerner accustomed to occupational safety precautions and regulations, the conditions in these plants are horrific. Workers breathe asbestos dust all day with only a gauze mask for protection from the carcinogenic fibers. I wondered, as I photographed the men working amidst the eerie white dust, whether my health might be affected. My doctor later reassured me that asbestos-related disease develops after prolonged exposure, and may not develop until forty years later. Given my age, I wasn't too worried, but I realized that the workers in the plant would probably not be so fortunate.

We left the western regions for Xilinhot, in Inner Mongolia, to spend some time in the land of Kublai Khan's descendants, before heading to Xanadu, present-day Shangdu. We hoped to see herds of the famous Mongolian horses that so impressed Marco, and helped the Mongols create the biggest empire the world has ever known. But instead of vast pastures where noble steeds grazed and galloped, we found only parched and arid tracts, and no horses in sight, not to mention a scarcity of Mongolians themselves. An enduring drought has created a wasteland, leaving hundreds of starving horses that horsemen have been forced to sell to the glue factory or that have wound up as a meal on someone's table.

Just as we had given up on locating any

horses or Mongolians to photograph, we came upon a fortunate herdsman with 200 horses on the day of his annual spring round-up. We got to watch an ancient form of horse roping, as the Mongolian cowboys lassoed the horses using long bamboo poles with rope loops on the end. The horsemen would snag the horses around the necks, then wrestle them down to the ground by their tails to brand and medicate them.

After this glimpse of life in Inner Mongolia, we moved on to Shangdu, Marco's final destination, where Kublai Khan reigned three months of the year from his fabled summer pleasure palace, immortalized by Samuel Taylor Coleridge's poem. Though it lives on in literature, all that is left of the Great Khan's marble palace now is rubble marking the barest outline of its layout, and shards of colored tiles, in brilliant blues, greens, reds and yellows, scattered about the grounds.

It was here Marco Polo became a trusted confidant and spent 17 years in service to Kublai Khan. In his work for the emperor, he traveled to the farthest reaches of the Mongol empire, reporting on conditions far afield, all the while gathering the information that would enrich his book.

FROM KASHGAR TO XANADU

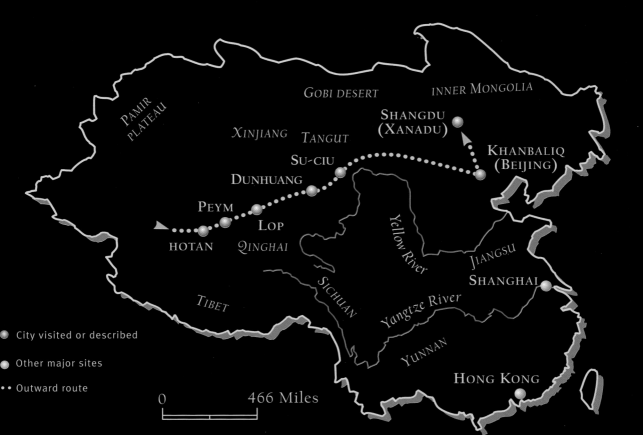

GOBI DESERT

INNER MONGOLIA

PAMIR PLATEAU

SHANGDU
(XANADU)

XINJIANG   TANGUT

KHANBALIQ
(BEIJING)

SU-CIU

DUNHUANG

PEYM

LOP

HOTAN   QINGHAI

Yellow River

JIANGSU

SHANGHAI

SICHUAN

Yangtze River

TIBET

YUNNAN

HONG KONG

- City visited or described
- Other major sites
- Outward route

0   466 Miles

YARKAND
CULTIVATING THE DESERT

"Everything is to be had in plenty, including abundance of cotton, [with flax, hemp, wheat, wine, and the like]. The people have vineyards and gardens and estates. They live by commerce and manufactures, and are no soldiers."

The Travels of Marco Polo, *Vol. I, Bk. 1, Ch. 36*

262-263 Planting cotton seeds.

264 In the Hotan region, spinning silk is still performed using large spinning wheels.

265 Even the boiling of the cocoons is carried out using a long-established method.

Hotan
The hawks of Xinjiang

"The people are Idolaters, and possess plenty of camels and cattle, and the country produces a number of good falcons, both Sakers and Lanners."

The Travels of Marco Polo, *Vol. I, Bk. 1, Ch. 45*

266-267 A falconer shows off his pride and joy.

268-269 Examination and sale of jade from the bed of the river Yurungkax, near Hotan.

270-271 Sandstorm in Gansu.

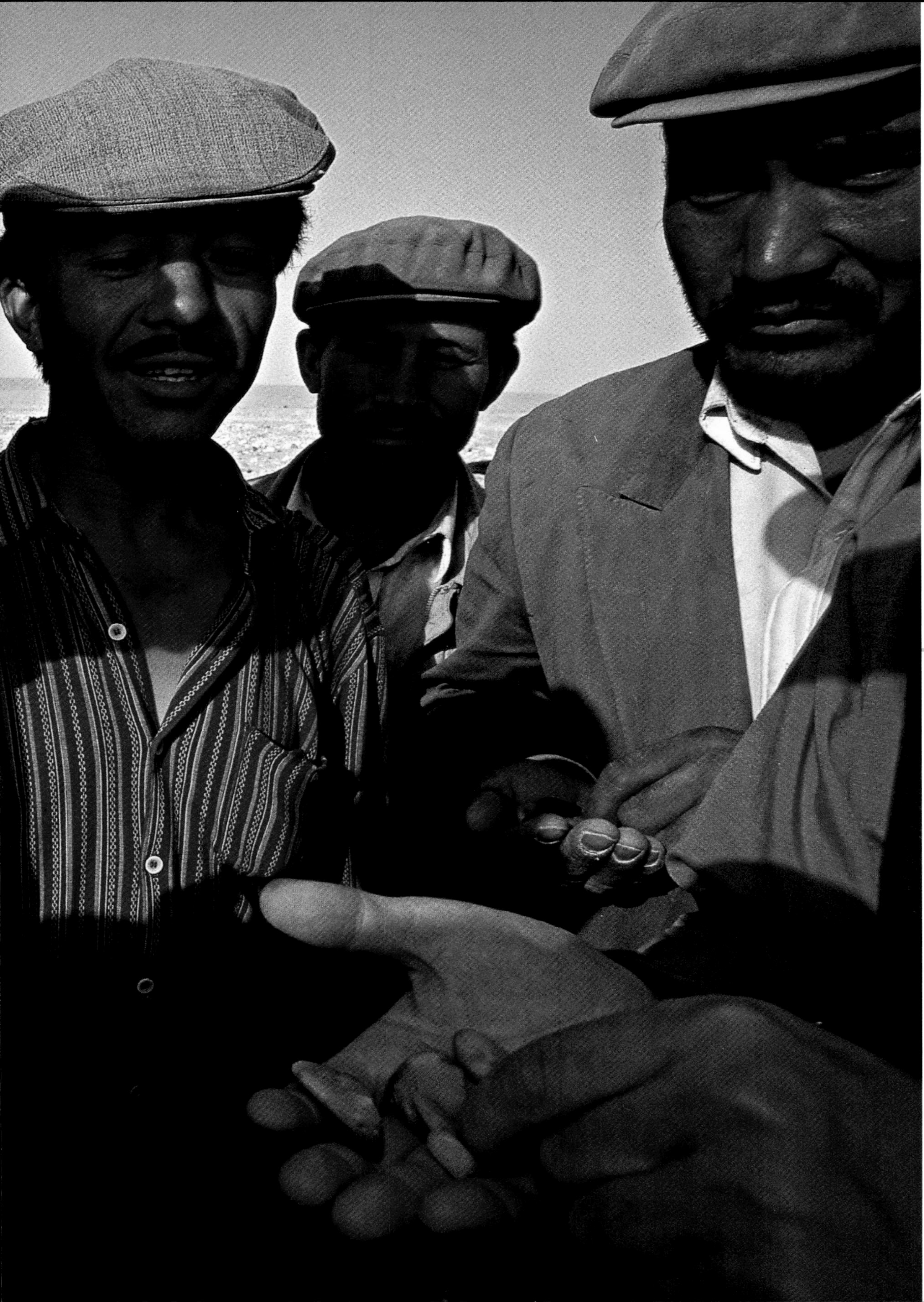

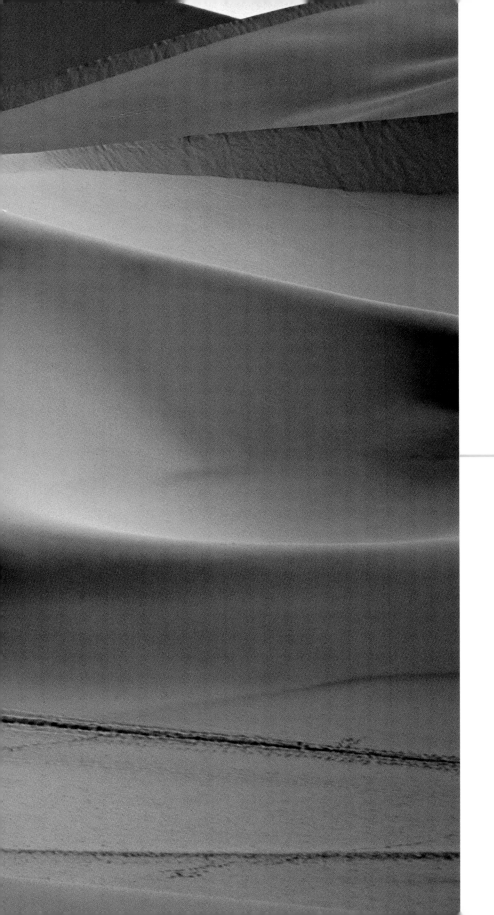

Taklimakan
The Sands that Sing

"When travellers are on the move by night, and one of them chances to lag behind [...] when he tries to gain his company again he will hear spirits talking, and will suppose them to be his comrades, [...] and thus shall a traveller of times be led astray so that he never finds his party. And in this way many have perished."

The Travels of Marco Polo, *Vol. I, Bk. 1, Ch. 39*

272-273 The 'Sands that Sing' form immense dunes.

THE MOGAO CAVES

274-275 A reclining Buddha in Mogao Caves. The Buddhist art in this site was created between the fifth and eighth centuries.

275 Mogao oasis was 'rediscovered' in the early twentieth century.

The Hexi Corridor

*"Travellers, however, dare not visit those
mountains with any cattle [...] for a certain
plant grows there which is so poisonous that
cattle which eat lose their hoofs. [...]
The people live by agriculture and have not
much trade. They are of a brown complexion.
The whole of the province is healthy"*

The Travels of Marco Polo, *Vol. I, Bk. 1, Ch. 43*

276-277 A hairy Bactrian camel is used
instead of an ox to plow a field in Gansu.

278-279 The Great Wall in Gansu.

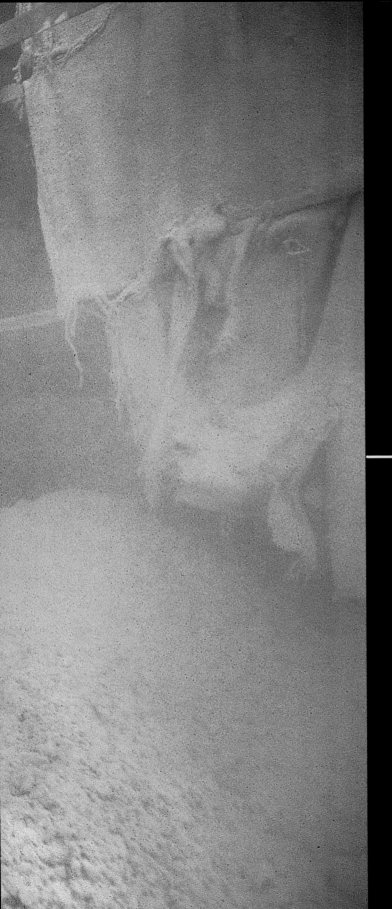

ASBESTOS
"THE CLOTH THAT DOESN'T BURN"

*"When first made these napkins are
not very white, but by putting them
into the fire for a while they come
out as white as snow. And so again
whenever they become dirty they are
bleached by being put in the fire".*

The Travels of Marco Polo, *Vol. I, Bk. 1, Ch. 42*

280-281 Dangerous asbestos dust pollutes
the air around a worker in Zhangye.

It is a fact that all over the country Cathay there is a kind of black stone existing in beds in the mountains, which they dig out and burn like firewood."

The Travels of Marco Polo, *Vol. I, Bk. 2, Ch. 30*

FOSSIL COAL
FIRE WITHOUT FLAMES

282 and 283 The Qilian Mountains have rich coal
reserves, as first cited by Marco Polo.

INNER MONGOLIA
THE HORSES OF THE KHAN

"*Every Lord or person who possesses beasts has them marked with his peculiar brand, be they horses, mares, camels, oxen, cows, or other great cattle, and then they are sent abroad to graze over the plains without any keeper.*"

The Travels of Marco Polo, *Vol. I, Bk. 1, Ch. 55*

284-285 The demanding task of breaking a colt, Mongolian style.

CHINA

FROM BEIJING TO JIANGSU

Next to luck, timing is everything for a photographer.

The two usually work hand in hand. They certainly did when I was trying to illustrate the section of Marco's book on the Yangtze River. Marco noted that there were more boats on the Yangtze than in all of Europe. My first impression of this mighty 3625-mile long river, whose waters alternately nourish and devastate the plains of central China, was disappointing.

Today the Yangtze is plied primarily by large barges, instead of the graceful junks with billowing rectangular sails that Marco would have seen. Still intent on a picture, we went on to Yangzhou, the city where Marco Polo supposedly lived for three or four years as a bureaucrat working for Kublai Khan's government.

In Yangzhou, we headed for the Grand Canal, a manmade waterway described by Marco that travels nearly 1100 miles from Beijing through eastern China and passes by the Yangtze as it proceeds south to Hangzhou. The river gods were smiling on us that day, as we found the waters of the canal at the confluence of the Yangtze engulfed by boats of all sizes. One of the locks that regulate river traffic and water flow had a breakdown, flooding my viewfinder with nothing but boats.

One aspect of this assignment I greatly liked was that it differed from the many magazine shoots on China I had worked on in the past. These had been dedicated to the modern and high-tech, from Beijing to Guangzhou and the affluent southern regions. Marco gave me a chance to show ancient China and to delve into the traditions of the empire. I photographed the contemplative gardens in Yangzhou and the canals of Suzhou (the 'Venice of the East'), which, like Marco's hometown, is one of the few cities of the world built on water. And then, too, in Suzhou, there was the 'Marco Polo Bridge', so-named because the Venetian described it in the thirteenth century exactly as it is today, with its single large arch, wide and tall enough to allow sailboats to pass under. When I photographed it, the morning mist, like a veil on an aging matron, hid the signs of the bridge's age; not to mention telephone wires and a modern barge.

Marco also described the famous West Lake in Hangzhou, with its bridges built three centuries before his arrival. He wrote at length about the activity along its banks, and the al fresco dining and diversions enjoyed by the ancient city's inhabitants, all unheard of by the Europeans of the day. Marco

THE GREAT WALL
AN ENDLESS RAMPART

287 Marco Polo never mentioned the Great Wall, leading some extreme critics to doubt his ever having been in China. However, the Wall only became continuous and "great" centuries later. Shown here is the Wall at Jinshaling, north of Beijing.

FROM BEIJING TO JIANGSU

PAMIR PLATEAU

GOBI DESERT

INNER MONGOLIA

XINJIANG

TANGUT

Yellow River

KHANBALIQ
(BEIJING)

QINGHAI

Grand Canal

YANGZHOU

SHANGHAI

JIANGSU

SICHUAN

Yangtze River

TIBET

QUINSAY
(HANGZHOU)

YUNNAN

City visited or described

Other major sites

0   466 Miles

Outward route

HONG KONG

depicts a people who dance and sing, and who have leisure time to devote to friends and family. In thirteenth-century Europe, not even the wealthiest merchants, much less the lower ranks, left their fortified cities to enjoy a picnic in the surrounding fields. In China, however, even commoners could indulge themselves in this sort of pleasure. Such detailed observations of a China far more civilized than Europe of the thirteenth century are one of the reasons the Chinese are such Marco Polo fans. In the ongoing game of international nose-thumbing, they are happy to support Marco's claim that Hangzhou, for example, was the largest and most advanced city in the world. Hangzhou's population exceeded one million, says Marco, while Paris at the time had just a little over 100,000, and London didn't reach this figure until six centuries later.

Hangzhou was also the only place in China where Marco gave a detailed description of native eating habits, discussing at length the lifestyle of the people who lived on the shores of the West Lake. Marco tells of the locals breeding in the lake the fish they ate, an early form of aquaculture unknown in the West in Marco's day; the day I photographed, fishermen were pulling silver carp they had farmed out of the lake. He also describes the amazing variety of meat, fish and vegetable dishes the Chinese ate, foods far more varied than seen on any table in thirteenth-century Europe.

Variety in dining is still a priority in modern China. A six-course meal — cold appetizers, a soup, a fish dish, a choice of meat courses, a vegetable, always followed by rice or noodles — is normal everyday fare, no matter how many are dining. Whenever I ate with my driver and my interpreter/guide, I always asked them not to order so many courses, as we invariably wound up with far more food on the table than we could eat. But my requests were usually ignored, as my traveling companions seemed more interested in a variety of tastes and textures than they were worried about too many leftovers.

Food, in general, is of prime importance to most Chinese. And though they are particular about quality and variety, the Chinese welcome diversity in dining. In other words, they'll eat just about anything that moves, or doesn't, for that matter. In the ancient capital of Nanking, I photographed a market stall that offered delicacies like live snakes, which the proprietors handle with skill and serve to discriminating shoppers. The market also included areas that sold dogs, cats, tortoises, rats, water bugs and scorpions and practically every other form of animal imaginable.

In spite of recent and continuing explosive growth, China, unlike many other nations, seems to be holding onto its traditions. With Marco's book in hand and modern China in front of me, it was fascinating to see just how little many things had changed in seven centuries.

THE MARCO POLO
BRIDGE
UNCHANGED BEAUTY

*"Over the river of Pulisanghin there is a
very fine stone bridge, so fine indeed, that it
has very few equals. [...] It is 300 paces in
length, and it must have a good eight paces
of width, for ten mounted men can ride
across it abreast."*

The Travels of Marco Polo, *Vol. II, Bk. 2, Ch. 35*

290-291 The omnipresent bicycles in Beijing
crowd the Marco Polo Bridge.

YANGZHOU

"So that this Yanju is, you see, a city of great
importance. And Messer Marco Polo himself,
of whom this book speaks, did govern this city
for full years, by the order of the Great Kaan."

The Travels of Marco Polo,
Vol. II, Bk. 2, Ch. 68

292-293 Lake Shouxi in Yangzhou is a series of
bridges, man-made islands and pavilions.

THE GRAND CANAL
YANGZHOU

*"There pass and repass on its waters a
great number of vessels, and more wealth
and merchandize than on all the rivers
and all the seas of Christendom put
together! [...] Polo said that he once beheld
at that city 15,000 vessels at one time."*

The Travels of Marco Polo,
Vol. II, Bk. 2, Ch. 71

294-295 Hundreds of boats create an
immense traffic jam on the Grand Canal
in Yangzhou.

296   Suzhou's numerous canals have earned the city the name of 'The Venice of the East.'

CHINESE OPERA
MUSIC ON THE WATER

298-299 Chinese opera enthusiasts rehearse in a pavilion on the canal built by Emperor Qian Long.

LAKE SHOUXI
WHERE TIME STOPS

*"For on the side lies the city in its entire
length, so that the spectators in the barges,
from the distance at which they stand,
take in the whole prospect in its full beauty
and grandeur, with its numberless palaces,
temples, monasteries, and gardens, full of
lofty trees, sloping to the shore.*

The Travels of Marco Polo,
Vol. II, Bk. 2, Ch. 77

300-301 Fishing in the tranquil waters
of the Shouxi Lake in Yangzhou.

THE GRAND CANAL
SUZHOU'S MAINSTREET

"You must know that the vessels on this river, in going up-stream have to be tracked, for the current is so strong that they could not make head in any other manner. Now the tow-line, which is some 300 paces in lenght, is made nothing but cane."

The Travels of Marco Polo,
Vol. II, Bk. 2, Ch. 71

302-303 Sunset in Suzhou sets the water of the Grand Canal alight.

FISH FARMING
ON THE WEST LAKE

"There is also great store of fish from the lake, which is the constant resort of fishermen, who have no other business. Their fish is of sundry kinds, changing with the season; and, owing to the impurities of the city which pass into the lake, it is remarkably fat and savoury."

The Travels of Marco Polo,
Vol. II, Bk. 2, Ch. 77

304-305 Fisherman with their haul on the West Lake in Hangzhou, where aquaculture has been practiced since the Middle Ages.

"And you must know that in this city there are 6,000 bridges, all of stone, and so lofty that a galley, or even two galleys at once, could pass underneath one of them."

The Travels of Marco Polo, *Vol. II, Bk. 2, Ch. 75*

TIME'S VEIL
ENCHANTED WATERS

306 Practicing *tai chi* in a pavilion on the West Lake.

306-307 Mist erases all indications of time around the
Marco Polo Bridge, Suzhou.

THE SUN'S MANSION
THE LAKE OF THE POET-RULERS

309   Sunset dissolves the blue of the lovely West Lake.

"*When they come to the burning place, they take representations of things cut out of parchment, such as caparisoned horses, [...] slaves, camels, armour, suits of cloth of gold (and money). [...] And they tell you that the dead man shall have all these [...] which effigies are burnt, alive in flesh and blood [...] in the next world.*"

The Travels of Marco Polo, *Vol. II, Bk. 2, Ch. 76.*

TAO IS IN THE AIR
SMOKE PRAYERS

310 and 311 Incense and ritual 'lucky charm' banknotes are burned in the Taoist temple.

MICHAEL YAMASHITA

CHINA

SICHUAN, YUNNAN, LAOS AND MYANMAR

T O BE OBJECTIVE IN OUR COVERAGE, AND AT THE RISK OF GIVING FUEL TO THOSE WHO DOUBT WHETHER MARCO'S STORY REALLY IS A FIRST-HAND ACCOUNT OF AN ACTUAL JOURNEY, WE HAD TO SHOOT THINGS HE PROBABLY SAW, BUT FAILED TO MENTION IN HIS BOOK.

One of the many traditions that Marco must have witnessed but never commented on was tea drinking. So I documented tea processing at a factory in the city of Yaan, southwest of Chengdu, the capital of Sichuan province. Much harder to find, but truly a living relic of the ancient China that Marco knew, was the practice of foot binding.

When we asked our guide for help in finding women with bound feet, she refused on the grounds that foot binding is an ancient custom that belong to a past that Communist China no longer recognizes. A custom of the elite classes, it is rarely spoken of anymore and considered cruel and humiliating to women.

In order to create the desired effect — exaggeratedly small feet — girls between the ages of three and ten would have their feet wrapped in extremely tight bandages, which gradually contorted the bone structure. The big toe was left pointing forward and the other four toes were bent under the sole of the foot, making it diffi-

cult to walk with more than short, mincing steps. Though Marco never mentioned the actual process of binding, he did note the distinctive way Chinese women walked, with extremely tiny steps.

We knew there could only be a few women with bound feet still alive, and those who were had to be in their late 70s or 80s, as the practice was banned at the turn of the last century. Though it quickly died out in the cities, it took longer to disappear in rural areas.

Through our own research, we learned of a village in Yunnan province where a famous dance group, the "Little Feet Dance Company," was performing. Our guide again refused to take us there, but fortunately we had another English-speaking (male) assistant who agreed to accompany us to the village to translate for us. We left the hotel and hurriedly flagged down a cab, telling the driver we wanted to visit the village where we could find the Little Feet Dance Company. The young man gave us a large smile, "I was born there! And my grandmother has the smallest feet in the village." Our luck was holding.

The man took us to his birthplace, where we met his grandmother and her dearest friend, who also had "little" feet. Rather than seeming ashamed or saddened by her condition, she was clearly proud of her rank among the women in

THE TRIBES OF THE HILLS

A woman from the Yao ethnic group displays a dazzling set of gold tee

Bagan, Myanmar
The valley of a thousand temples

214 The skimming light floods the valley of Bagan with gold

village. She boasted about her feet, and she and her friend were happy to talk to us and pose for pictures. If the practice had caused her suffering, she did not show it. For her, the tradition was more a badge of honor than a barbaric custom.

In Yunnan we met with two other surprises. In this beautiful province of towering mountains and deep gorges, where three mighty rivers (the Mekong, the Yangtze and Salween) flow within several miles of each other, Marco described a people living on the shores of Lake Erhai who ate raw meat. This we had to see.

The system we used to track down details mentioned by Marco was simple: we would arrive at our destination and through our interpreters ask for what we were looking for. If the answer was "no, never heard of it," we would move on to the next town or city and start up with the usual questions once more. This approach was not only effective, but also entertaining, as sometimes we got more than we asked for. Near the village where we found the raw meat eaters, Marco had mentioned that there were people in the habit of implanting gold teeth and tattooing themselves. In our hunt, we were besieged by women whose wide smiles revealed sets of sparkling golden teeth and by young men who happily lifted their shirts to show us their ornate tattoos.

Then finally someone told us that raw meat was still eaten in the village where we were, but only on special occasions like weddings, anniversaries and festivals. We asked for more

precise information from a boy who, surprisingly, replied in perfect English. He was a student at the university in Kunming, the provincial capital of Yunnan, and had returned to his village to attend a wedding. When we asked him if the wedding would include a banquet with raw meat, he told us, "Of course. Come tomorrow at six when the pigs will be slaughtered." Marco hadn't mentioned that the meat was pork!

We were there at six sharp, ready to shoot the ritual, which seemed to be eagerly awaited by all those in attendance. Soon three large pigs were brought out and slaughtered. Shrieking as their throats were slit, their blood spurted everywhere, as the wedding guests, who had already started celebrating, danced and drank with gusto. After the animals had been bled, they were placed over a straw fire just long enough to burn the hairs from their skin. The carcasses were cut open, and as a precaution, a portion of the meat was taken away by a health official to check for trichinosis. Many of the revelers couldn't wait for the results, but instead dove in, tearing and hacking off pieces of meat from the belly and eating them raw on the spot.

The women prepared the rest of the meat by cutting it into tiny cubes, then mixing it with garlic and chili peppers. Once again, Marco was surprisingly accurate in describing an almost identical meal at which the meat was flavored with garlic and chili peppers. We were invited to join in the feasting, which we did, and all I can say about traditional Yunnan raw pork is that it tastes mainly of garlic and chili peppers.

Our next stop was Myanmar, formerly known as Burma. Before arriving in Myanmar, however, we faced a dilemma. The pages of my passport were filled with journalist stamps and visas. But the Myanmar government wasn't keen on visiting members of the press. So I requested a replacement passport free of any journalistic stamps. I then presented the new one to the Myanmar embassy six months later to get my authorization. A few days later I was in Bagan, which Kublai Khan had conquered shortly before Marco's arrival in Myanmar.

Throughout our trip, we had been using Marco's book as a tourist guide, underlining the places, people and customs we wanted to document, and then heading to the location to find them. That it hadn't been updated in seven centuries and could still be used this way was our major motivation for the trip and a source of great satisfaction every time we came upon one of Marco's "finds."

Coming upon the hundreds of sparkling Buddhist temples that are spread across the Bagan valley —the Temples of Gold, as Marco described them — was one of those "eureka!" moments. Together, these temples comprise the largest existing Buddhist stupa site in the world. Polo described the forest of dazzling gold towers rising above the rolling hills of central Myanmar, and again the challenge was to convey the same sensation that Marco must have felt as he saw them for the first time, far removed from the twentieth century.

A friend who had recently visited Bagan told me about a new hot-air ballooning outfit that took tourists on a flight over the valley, called BOB, for Balloons Over Bagan. I figured that floating over the hills and valley in a balloon would provide me with the temple views I needed. And I was right.

Balloonists only fly in ideal weather conditions, either at sunrise or sunset, all equally advantageous for photographers. I was to fly with an internationally known pilot, Jackie Hibberd, famed for her skill as a balloonist. We scheduled a morning and afternoon flight. The first flight was idyllic. We lifted off and glided silently over the valley, with only the slight whoosh of the gas jets as accompaniment. It was amazing to see the golden towers from above, as well as the everyday life going on below us. After an easy landing, we all toasted our success with the traditional bottle of Champagne.

The afternoon ride was a different story. The wind had shifted, and the pilot informed me that we were getting very little lift. That meant that we couldn't fly as high as we had earlier. It also meant that we got unusually, and occasionally uncomfortably, close to those spectacular stupas, not to mention trees and houses. Landing wasn't much better, as the search car had to scramble to find our balloon. But with Jackie's expert handling, we made it back to our base with the pictures I'd been aiming for, and in time for another glass of Champagne.

SICHUAN, YUNNAN, LAOS AND MYANMAR

PAMIR PLATEAU

GOBI DESERT

XINJIANG

Yellow River

KHANBALIQ (BEIJING)

QINGHAI

XI'AN

CHENGDU

SICHUAN

JIANGSU

SHANGHAI

TIBET

Yangtze River

Erhai Lake

YUNNAN

HONG KONG

BAGAN

MYANMAR

LAOS

YANGON

VIENTIANE

- City visited or described
- Other major sites
- Outward route

0   466 Miles

LESHAN
THE GREAT BUDDHA

318 The sacred Mount Leshan in Sichuan has the largest stone
Buddha in the world.

319 The Leshan Buddha's head alone is an amazing 48 feet in height.

YAAN
THE AVENUES OF THE KHAN

321

"The Emperor moreover hath taken order that all the highways travelled by his messengers and the people generally should be planted with rows of great trees a few paces apart. [...] Even the roads through uninhabited tracts are thus planted, and it is the greatest possible solace to travellers."

The Travels of Marco Polo,
Vol. I, Bk. 2, Ch. 28

320-321 Morning traffic on an avenue in Yaan in Sichuan province.

Tea harvest
The green gold of China

322-323 Harvesting *pekoe,* the tender
tea leaves, in Yunnan.

The tea of Yaan

324 Tea production in a factory in Yaan.

325 Final phase of tea-leaf processing in the Yaan factory.

Foot binding in Yunnan
What Marco left untold

The shoes on the left, looking like those of a toddler, belong to an eighty-year-old woman, whose feet were bound when she was a child.

327   Abolished for decades, the feet of elderly ladies are sometimes still marked by binding.

Lugu
The Lamas' Lake

"There is a lake here, in which are found pearls [which are white and not round]. But the Great Kaan will not allow them to be fished. [...] Only when it is his pleasure they take from the lake. [...] but anyone attempting to take them on his own account would be incontinently put to death."

The Travels of Marco Polo,
Vol. II, Bk. 2, Ch. 47

328-329 Women of the Mosuo minority are rowing towards the Lugu Lake monastery, in Yunnan.

Erhai Lake
Fishing with cormorants

"There is a lake in this country of a good hundred miles in compass, in which are found great quantities of the best fish in the world; fish of great size of all sorts."

The Travels of Marco Polo,
Vol. II, Bk. 2, Ch. 48

330-331 Marco Polo doesn't mention this centuries-old tradition, still practiced.

YUNNAN
THE RAW FLESH EATERS

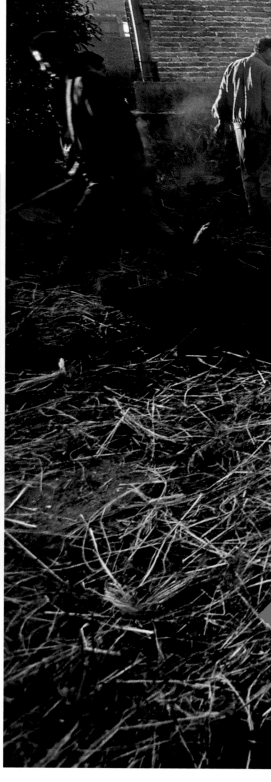

332 and 333 Preparation of a wedding banquet in the village of Shazun, Yunnan. The pig is placed on the fire to burn off the bristles, then eaten raw.

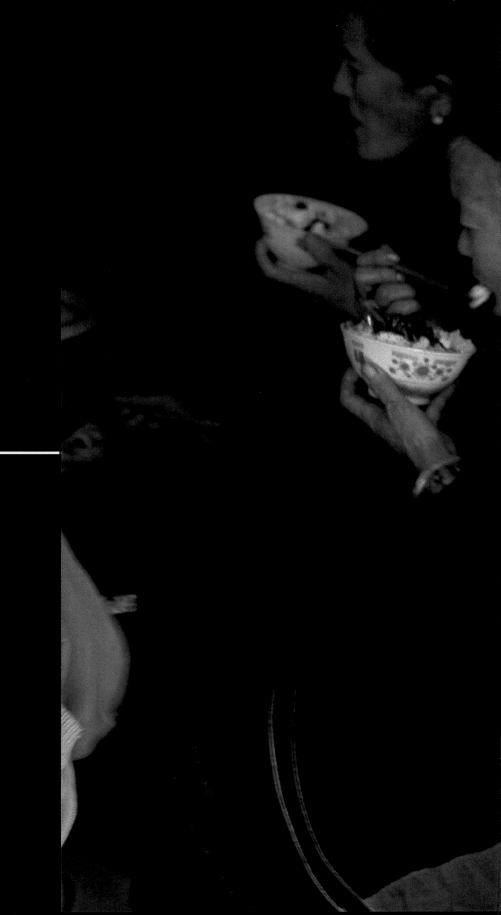

SHAZUN

LIFE IN THE VILLAGE

*"People of that country eat their meat raw,
whether it be mutton, beef, buffalo, poultry,
or any other kind [...] and put it in a sauce
of garlic and spices, and so eat it; and
other meat in like manner, raw, just as we
eat meat that is dressed."*

The Travels of Marco Polo,
Vol. II, Bk. 2, Ch. 48

334-335 A communal meal in the village of Shazun.

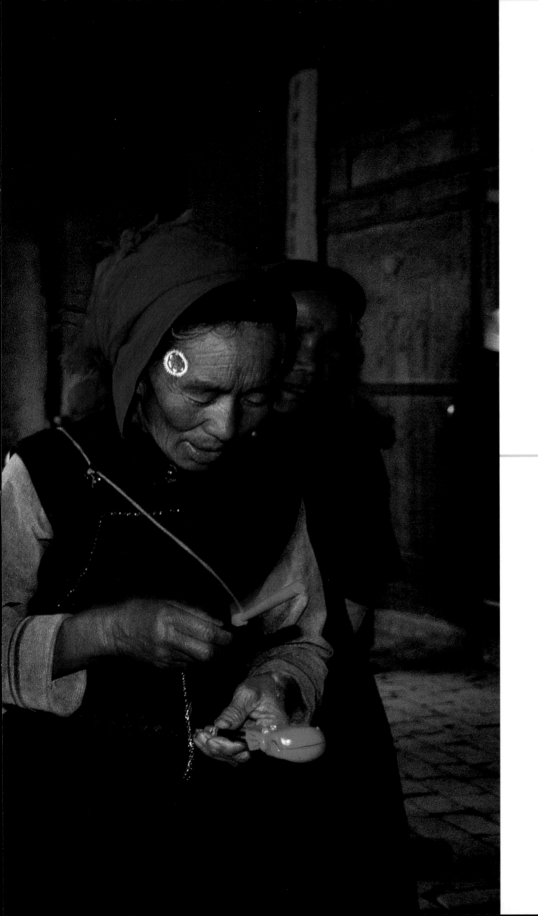

Quindong, Dali
Rain and prosperity

336-337 Bai women from Qindong, near Lake Erhai, pray for rain after planting rice.

338-339 A traditional Bai house overlooks the quiet landscape of ricefields in Xizhou, Yunnan.

YUNNAN
THE RICE LAND

340 and 341 Bai women transplant rice for one of the annual harvests.

ZHOUCHANG
THE BAI MARKET

342-343 Burdened with vegetables, this Bai woman is off to the market on the banks of Erhai Lake.

344-345 Back to the stable. The Mekong river has chiseled gorges as deep as 9,900 feet.

Mekong
The Mother of waters

"The river [...] is so big that no bridge can be thrown across it; for it is of immense width and depth, and reaches to the Great Ocean that encircles the Universe, - I mean the whole earth."

The Travels of Marco Polo,
Vol. II, Bk. 2, Ch. 40

346-347 In Lanping, Yunnan, the Mekong river divides rice fields from bare slopes.

"They find in this country a good deal of gold, and they also have great abundance of spices. But they are such a long way from the sea that the products are of little value. They live on flesh and milk and rice, and have wine made of rice and good spices."

The Travels of Marco Polo,
Vol. II, Bk. 2, Ch. 56

348

348-349 Rice sifting in Pak Beng, village not far from the Mekong river's big Laotian loop.

350-351 During the
inland drought, young
Myanmar women sift the
Mekong's waters,
panning for gold.

BAGAN
TOWERS OF SILVER
AND GOLD

"The King caused these towers to be erected to commemorate his magnificence and for the good of his soul; [...], so splendid and costly. And when they are lighted up by the sun they shine most brillantly and are visible from a vast distance."

The Travels of Marco Polo,
Vol. II, Bk. 2, Ch. 54

352-353 Sunset gives Bagan a mysterious timeless charm.

354-355 Bagan is also called "Valley of the Thousand Temples," but in the Middle Ages there were 13,000 stupas.

MICHAEL YAMASHITA

CHINA

LABRANG AND THE TIBETAN PLATEAU

T RAVELING AS A JOURNALIST HAS DEFINITE ADVANTAGES, PRIME AMONG THEM BEING ACCESS TO PLACES AND PEOPLE THE AVERAGE TRAVELER WOULD NEVER SEE OR MEET.

However, it does have some distinct disadvantages, especially as international relations grow increasingly tense. Case in point: Tibet. The Chinese government did not want me to travel in Tibet, although they do allow tourists to visit this Himalayan land with its nomads, a unique form of Buddhism, and the Dalai Lama.

Marco reports extensively on this kingdom at the roof of the world, so there was no question that I had to go there, but getting the necessary permissions to enter Tibet was impossible. Our fall-back was Labrang, which in Marco Polo's time stood on Tibetan territory, when the borders of the country were much more extensive. Labrang is now in China, in Gansu province, and is the largest Buddhist monastery outside of Tibet.

Marco Polo described a monastery much like Labrang, with two thousand resident monks. Today the imposing monastic complex is like a religious college, where hundreds of monks still live and worship, studying the Buddhist arts, philosophy and traditions, though the 'lessons' we witnessed seemed more like stylized rituals than classroom academics.

We were moved by the spectacle of the monks in their crimson robes and golden hats curved like rams' horns. We were also struck by the devotion and spirituality at Labrang, not only of the monks, but by secular Tibetans, whose religion invests everything they do.

Everywhere we went we were treated with extreme kindness, especially by the Tibetans who had come to worship in this sacred place. Hundreds of pilgrims cross the border from the Chinese province of Tibet to reach Labrang in Gansu. I watched in amazement as those pilgrims performed one of the most profoundly reverent acts of worship I have ever seen.

Just as Marco recounted, fervent Tibetans prostrate themselves completely with their faces in the dust and arms and legs outstretched, then they kneel, rise to their feet, bow deeply with their hands together, and finally stretch themselves out on the ground once more.

This act takes them forward a distance about

Mountain Corals

357 A woman from Xiahe adorns her embroidered silk dress with a heavy necklace o

City visited or described

Other major sites

0   640 Miles

LABRANG AND THE TIBETAN PLATEAU

359 Heedless of the blizzard, the monks at Labrang await the start of morning prayers.

twice their height, roughly ten feet. They proceed this way for tens of miles, yard after yard, intent on a journey that leads to a state of blessedness, though it is a pilgrimage that may take several lives to complete. These pilgrims of the twenty-first century are all dressed in the same way as their medieval predecessors and perform the same rituals. Time as we know it has no meaning in Labrang.

I had come to Labrang during the New Year celebrations to photograph the 'Dancing Devils' that Marco wrote about and is now a great tourist attraction. Marco would never have guessed that my biggest problem would be to keep other photographers out of my shots. It was not the only difficulty, however; another obstacle was the monks whose duty it was to control the crowds. They would strike out at the spectators with their sticks, regardless of whether they were Tibetans or foreigners. Their role as temple "bouncers" was to keep the column of spectators moving. Anyone holding up the line would be swatted with the sticks. I paid the price of several wallops for the photographs I managed to get.

Having rung in the Tibetan New Year, it was time to head for Quanzhou.

QINGHAI
THE HIMALAYAN SPURS

360-361 Dawn in Qinghai reveals the
Tibetan Plateau's dramatically beautiful
skyline.

362-363 A wild donkey wanders across
the desert lands of Qinghai on the
Tibetan Plateau.

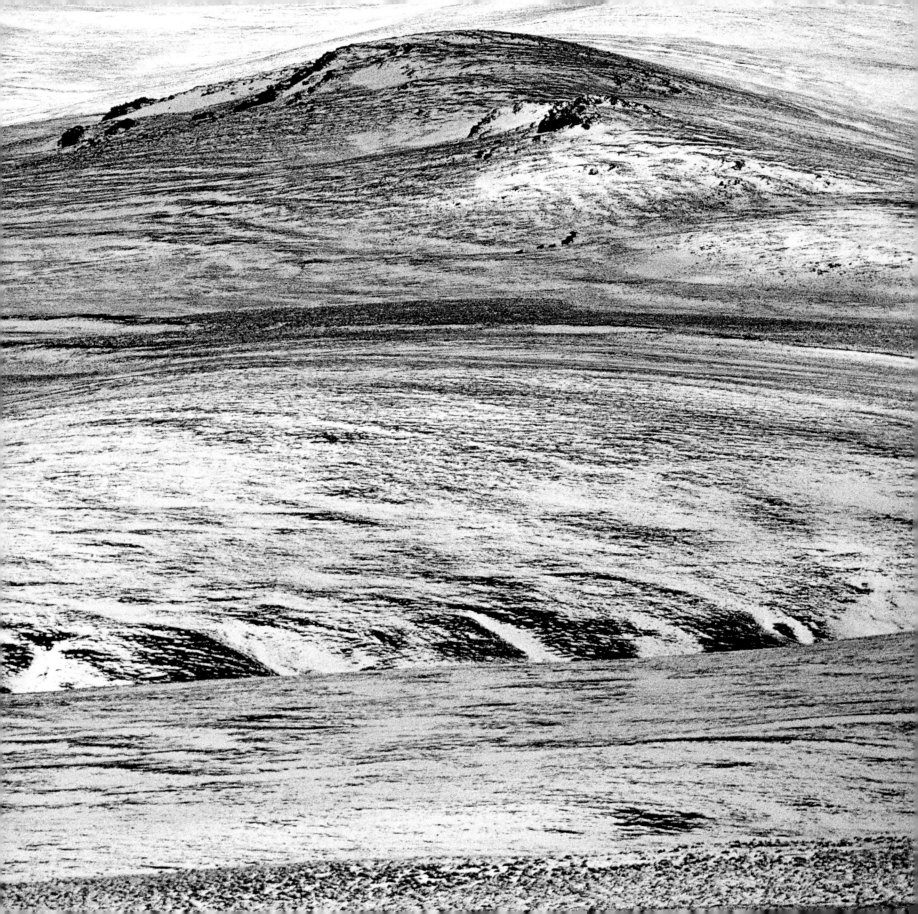

QINGHAI
TIBET OUTSIDE TIBET

"There are wild cattle in that country [almost] as big as elephants, splendid creatures, covered everywhere but on the back with shaggy hair a good four palms long."

The Travels of Marco Polo,
Vol. I, Bk. 1, Ch. 57

364-365 A woman in Qinghai province milking a dri, a female yak.

QINGHAI
THE SOURCE OF THE MEKONG

366-367 Making tea in a summer camp
near the source of the Mekong river.

ZADOI
GATEWAY TO TIBET

"They are very poorly clad, for their clothes are only of the skins of beasts, and of canvas, and of buckram. They have a language of their own, and they are called Tebet."

The Travels of Marco Polo,
Vol. II, Bk. 2, Ch. 45

368-369 Kids in Zadoi divide their time between
school and yak-tending. Yaks are the only things of
value their families own.

Xiahe
Women in Gansu

370-371 Tibetan worshippers crowd the entrance to the main temple.

MONLAM
NEW YEAR'S DAY IN XIAHE

372 In busy Xiahe, close to the Labrang monastery, youngsters in their finery prepare to celebrate Monlam, the Buddhist New Year.

373 A woman's elaborate hairstyle made use of coral and coins.

Labrang
The city of the monks

"They have also immense Minsters and Abbeys, some of them as big as a small town, with more than two thousand monks in a single abbey. These monks dress more decently than the rest of the people, and have the head and beard shaven."

The Travels of Marco Polo,
Vol. I, Bk. 1, Ch. 61

374-375 Monks of all ages wait for morning prayers and the only meal of the day.

Music school
The sound of the 'om

376-377 Music lesson for Labrang's monks
using the traditional 13-foot horns.

"*What they take is a certain fine white bast or skin which lies between the wood of the tree and the thick outer bark, and this they make into something resembling sheets of paper, but black. When these sheets have been prepared they are cut up into pieces of different sizes.*"

The Travels of Marco Polo,
Vol. I, Bk. 2, Ch. 24

378-379 In a room of the monastery the monks prepare the paper that will be used for the Buddhist *mantra*.

380 Monasticism is not just prayer: young monks intensively discuss the doctrine of the Enlightened One.

381 Monks quench their thirst with freshly fallen snow.

The ciak
Pilgrims' Progress

382-383 The *ciak* is probably the most demanding form of pilgrimage in the world. Prostrating themselves fully, worshippers cover tens, sometimes hundreds, of miles.

Labrang
Morning prayer

"[...] are men of extraordinary abstinence
after their fashion, and lead a life of such
hardship as I will describe. All their life
long they eat nothing but bran, which
they take mixt with hot water.
That is their food: bran and nothing but
bran; and water for their drink."

The Travels of Marco Polo,
Vol. I, Bk. 1, Ch. 61

384-385 The *trapa*, (novices) enter
the monastery around the age of six
and become *gelong* (monks) when
they reach adulthood.

Yellow hats
The Tsongkhapa lamas

386-387 The monks of Labrang belong to the sect known as 'yellow hats', founded by Tsongkhapa in the fourteenth-century A.D.

Monlam
A new year has started

"They make a great feast in honour of their god, and hold great ceremonies of worship with great illuminations. [...] Each of the idols has a name of his own, and a feast-day, just as our Saints have their anniversaries."

The Travels of Marco Polo,
Vol. I, Bk. 1, Ch. 61

388-389 On festival days, the monastery fills with monks, worshippers and tourists to watch the dancing in the center of the large square.

A thirst for holiness
Water from the Buddha's well

390-391 Holding out their bowls, worshippers wait
for holy water drawn from the Living Buddha's well.

392

392 and 393 Outside the monastery, many food stands sell
sunflower seed, soya beans and noodles.

THE SACRED TANGKHA
THE APPEARANCE OF THE ENLIGHTENED ONE

394 and 395 With cords providing control, the *tangkha* is then unfurled along a sloping wall.

396-397 Once unfurled, the colorful image is admired by the hundreds of people in the square.

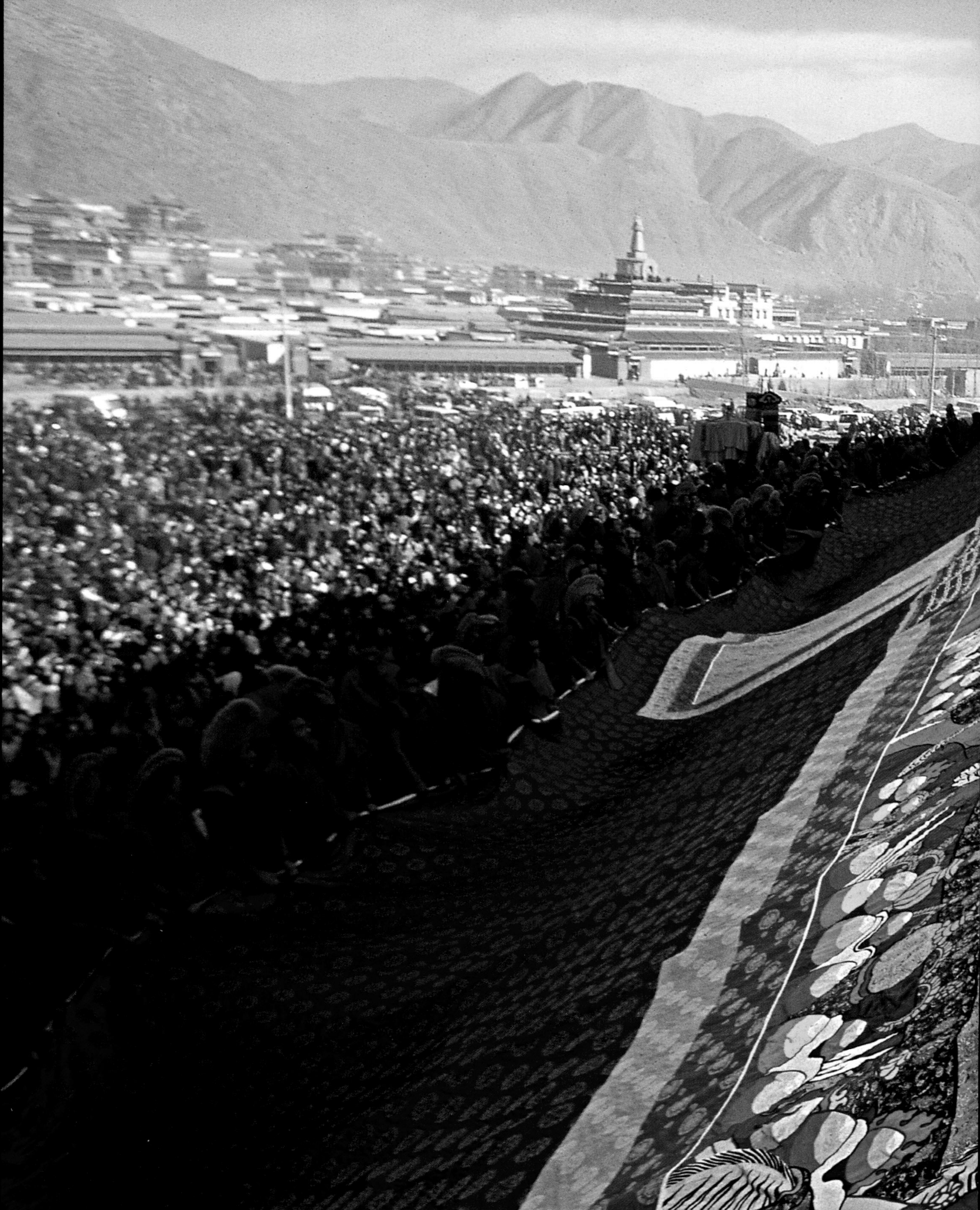

THE
RETURN
JOURNEY

INTRODUCTION

THE TRIPS MARCO MADE FOR KUBLAI KHAN WERE NOT LIMITED TO CHINA FOR, IN THAT PERIOD, THE GREAT MONGOL SOVEREIGN WAS EXTENDING HIS DOMINION TO NEIGHBORING TERRITORIES.

For example, he added to his empire the small vassal kingdoms of the Indochinese peninsula but he was unsuccessful in his attempt to subdue Japan (called Cipangu by Marco Polo), which was saved miraculously when the kamikaze ('divine wind') destroyed the Mongol fleet. The adventurous Venetian went to see these lands, which lay beyond the borders of China's southern most regions, Yunnan and Kwangsi, perhaps in the train of the army. He tells us he came down from the mountains following 'a great slope' that took two and a half days to descend, and which took him to the tropical jungle of the Salween and Mekong valleys. These were 'uninhabited and foul places' in the sense of being steep and difficult, and populated by rhinoceroses and elephants. It took two weeks of difficult walking to arrive in the Burmese capital of Myen, 'very grand and noble.'

Kublai had sent a bizarre force to conquer this area, composed exclusively of minstrels and tumblers from his court. Marco explained that the Khan had chosen these men to spite the pride of the king of Myen who had refused to become a vassal of the Mongol might. Kublai's choice was spot-on because it took just the blink of an eye for the cheerful bunch of clowns and jugglers to take the capital. Having conquered and humiliated the city, the entertainers discovered a marvel: the funerary monument of an ancient king, with two large towers, one lined with gold, the other with silver, in which a myriad of gold-and silver-plated bells tinkled to the movement of the wind. The entertainers were highly moved by beauty, or strangeness at least, and rather than follow the draconian orders of the Khan and raze the city to the ground to punish the presumption of the king of Myen, they sent a message describing the beauty of the monument and asking for instructions. And Kublai, like a good Mongol, did 'not touch anything belonging to a dead man' and gave the order to save the tomb. In the East, as in the West, clowns have

400 The Great Khan's fleet sets sail for Cipangu, where it was to be destroyed by a typhoon.

401 left Crafts and trade in a city in Cilicia (Little Armenia).

401 right The Polo brothers try to convince Kublai to let them return home.

more sense than soldiers.

The years passed but there was no mention of return home though no doubt the Polos spoke of it amongst themselves when they met up after their respective travels; Kublai, however, did not seem willing to lose such valuable aids. It was luck that provided the three Venetians with the chance they had not dared to hope for.

While Marco was away from the capital on a mission to the coastal provinces of China, a diplomatic mission arrived in Khanbaliq that had set off from the distant land of Persia where Argun Khan ruled. The mission brought bad news: Bolgana, Kublai's great-niece and Argun's wife, had died, and the ambassadors were charged with asking the Grand Khan for the hand of another princess of the same

line. It was Argun's wish to strengthen the ties between the two dynasties, and Bolgana herself had given her husband the same advice as she lay on her deathbed.

Kublai was happy to comply. Argun's new bride was to be Princess Koekoecin, a beautiful seventeen-year-old whose name meant 'blue.' The caravan of envoys started off on the Silk Road that the Polos had followed on their journey to Khanbaliq fifteen or so years earlier. But after a few months, the Persians reappeared at the court of the Grand Khan because central Asia had been thrown into confusion by war and the convoy did not think it wise to proceed and put the princess's life at risk.

At that time, Marco reappeared in the imperial capital after a sea journey up the Chinese coast. The

Persians and Venetians, equally desirous of returning home, met to discuss the situation. The Polos suggested sailing as far as the Persian port of Hormuz, where the spice maritime routes began. Nothing could be easier insisted Marco, who had experience of the solidity and comfort of Chinese junks. Argun's ambassadors convinced Kublai to take this route, but in the company of the three Polos. Kublai agreed and gave the Venetians not just the usual passes of safe-conduct, but also letters for the Pope and for the kings of some other European nations.

The large party was made up of the princess and her retinue of maids and maids of honor, the ambassadors with their servants, an armed escort and the three Venetians, not to mention a phenomenal amount of baggage. They followed the roads and canals of half China as far as the city of Zaiton (modern-Guangzhou) 'where all the ships of India arrive with great cargoes of precious stones and other things, like large and good pearls.' It was from here that the Arab merchants took back costly and rare goods to the lands of Islam and Europe, and it was here that the party of travelers was awaited by a fleet of fourteen junks. These were the largest ships of the Middle Ages, much bigger than the contemporary ships in Europe, and provided with every comfort. There were spacious cabins with bathrooms, provisions of all kinds, including live animals, and soil in large boxes so as to grow fresh vegetables. The largest junks were able to hold a thousand people and their baggage; they had four decks, six masts and a dozen bamboo sails from which painted dragons fluttered. The large floating towns seemed unsinkable, but the ferocious typhoons of the eastern seas were to test the expedition; there were, in fact, very few survivors who reached Hormuz.

The fleet departed in 1291. The route lay south-west to circumnavigate the Indochinese peninsula and reach the Indian Ocean. A stopover was made in the kingdom of Champa (part of Vietnam) whose sovereign was then a vassal of the Great Khan and paid an annual tribute of twenty elephants and a cargo of aloe wood. That lucky king, noted Marco, enjoyed the right to sleep with all the single girls in the country, not one of which could marry 'without the king first trying her.' And if he liked her, he could keep her or give her in marriage to one of his 'barons.' This custom meant that the king had 326 children, and Marco knew this for a fact, having counted them personally during a visit to the kingdom in either 1280 or 1285 (the codices do not agree).

The expedition next stopped at the island of Sumatra where Marco had already been. Here he appreciated the fish ('the best in the world'), the rice and the palm wine – but not the inhabitants who were 'bad people.' As they were forced to stop there for five months because of bad weather, he made everyone leave the ships to build fortifications of tree trunks where they would be protected from the attacks of the

402 Unloading merchant ships in Cambaet, today Cambay, on the coast of Gujarat.

403 Sumatran cannibals prepare to dine...

worst natives or the many wild animals. This was not being excessively prudent as cannibalism existed on the island in that the natives would hasten the death of those who had been deemed incurably sick by the soothsayers, then boil and eat them, even sucking the marrow from the bones. The remainder would be buried and left to the worms so that the soul would not be able to do great harm. The foreigners, however, did not expect that the natives would bother waiting for them to sicken before killing and eating them.

While in Sumatra, in the kingdom of Lambri, which might be what is referred to now as Achen, Marco procured some seeds of a red wood that was used to create dye for cloth. He took the seeds to Venice but was unable to make them grow 'because of the cold.' He was told that in the hills of the island, men lived who

had tails longer than a hand's span. These were in fact orangutans, which is Malaysian for 'men of the woods.'

Although he reports this strange news of tailed men impassively, Marco was proud of having unmasked a small fraud by the devious locals. They sold 'small wild men' that they had stuffed. They were in fact small monkeys whose fur had been shaved off and the skin 'cured with saffron and other things' to give them as human a look as possible.

The island was filled with botanical marvels like camphor trees and sago palms whose trunks were 'filled inside with flour' which was good for 'various pasta dishes'.

Finally the conditions improved and the junks were once more able to leave the dangerous and inhospitable shores. They passed through the Strait of Malacca and

404 top Dog-headed merchants from the Andaman Islands sell fruit and cereals, the main resources of their archipelago.

404 bottom The king of Malabar in southwest India, naked like his subjects, wears only a necklace of gems.

headed towards the huge island of Seilan or Ceylon (now Sri Lanka) 'which is the best island in the world of its size.' They went straight past the Nicobar and Andoman archipelagoes without stopping owing to the bad reputation of their inhabitants: those living in the Nicobar islands went naked and lived like animals, while those in the Andomans had the heads and teeth of dogs and were also cannibalistic. Marco's citation was the medieval reappearance of the Dog-Headed people recounted in classical antiquity, though then they had been located much farther north, toward the Arctic Circle.

Marco had even previously visited Seilan: the text of *Il Milione* suggests that in 1284 he had been part of a diplomatic mission sent by Kublai. The ruler of the island, which was renowned for its precious stones, owned an extraordinary ruby, as red as fire, as thick as an arm and as long as a hand. The Grand Khan would have given much to have had it, even 'the value of a good city' but the king could not be persuaded to part with it and Marco had to return to Khanbaliq empty-handed.

We do not know if the fleet, when it left the island, had already suffered some loss at sea or if it was still entire, but next it stopped on the Indian coast of Cora-mandel, a country governed by five kings, all brothers. Here the gulf was a paradise for pearl divers but only during the months of April and May; in the other months there were no pearls to be found. The divers were accompanied by wizards called abraiaman (Brahmins) whose task it was to put a spell on the fish so that they would not attack the divers. The charm worked, but only for a single day because at night the fish 'were once more freed' and so no-one fished for pearls at night.

In these regions 'there is no need for clothing' because the temperature was neither cold nor hot. Everyone went naked apart from the simple dhoti. Even the king went bare-chested 'save he wore other things' including a dhoti that was more beautiful than those of his subjects. He also wore a collar of precious stones 'that is worth two treasures' and from his neck hung a silk string with 104 large pearls and rubies. It was a rosary because each day he had to say 104 prayers to his idols. He had 500 wives and a proportionate number of children. When the king died, all his children were burned on the pyre with the body of their father apart from the first-born, whose duty it was to reign, while the others had to serve the new king in the Afterworld.

In this region and all India, the people worshipped the ox 'because they say it is a good thing' and no-one ate beef, in fact, they ate nothing but rice. Before eating they performed ablutions and were fastidious and superstitious because they didn't eat with their left hand and used their right to touch and hold things that were clean and beautiful. They drank from individually owned mugs but did not allow them to touch their lips, pouring the liquid in from above. If a stranger wanted to drink, they did not give him a mug but poured the water or wine into his hands.

India was a country filled with philosophers who immediately knew if a man or woman is good or bad just by looking, and they could predict the future by watching the flight of the birds.

Heading north up the Indian coast, the junks

flanked the kingdom of Multifili which was ruled by a wise widowed queen. This was a country where the mountains contained diamonds that were washed down to the valley during the rainy season. The mountains were populated by poisonous and gigantic serpents and anyone who wanted to search for diamonds had to face these creatures, so a shrewd method was devised in which the diamond-hunters approached the top of the ravines in which both the precious stones and gigantic serpents lay, and threw down pieces of meat. The white eagles that lived on the peaks would smell the meat, fly down and pick it up in their talons and fly up. The men then ran at the eagles to frighten them and the birds would fly away abandoning their meat. The men would then find the diamonds that had stuck to the pieces of meat.

Lar was a trading district but the market was only held if the conditions were right: for example, first they measured the shadow and if it was too long then it was necessary to wait; also, they looked to see if a tarantula was coming (there were many), and if it approached from the wrong direction, the market was not held at all. Lar was also a region of fakirs who were able to live up to 200 years. They went around completely naked without shame and would not kill any living thing, including ticks, lice or flies because they believed them to have souls. Nor did they eat anything green until it had dried out. They could fast for an entire year, taking nourishment only from bread and water.

In Cochin it was so hot that if you put an egg in a river, it would soon be cooked. Malabar was a land of pirates, and so too was Gujarat; every day a hundred boats would put out to 'go robbing the sea.'

Was it these pirates who so depleted the expedition, which perhaps was already weakened by storms during their long voyage?

406 top
A lover of gems and pearls, the king of Lar in India purchases valuables from two Brahmins.

406 bottom
The queen of Multifili observes diamonds being mined.

407 Black-skinned natives from Cochin in Kerala harvest ripe pepper.

We will never know but in Hormuz only one junk arrived carrying 18 of the original 600 sailors, one of the three Persian ambassadors, a single maid of honor, and, fortunately, the most important passenger, the princess Koekoecin. Plus of course the three Venetians who seemed to be quite untouchable.

In Hormuz, where it was so hot that 'one could hardly live,' the few survivors learnt that their two-year odyssey had all been in vain because Argun Khan had died and his place taken by his son, a child of tender years. But the links between the Mongol dynasties were too important to be disregarded, so a straightforward solution was found: the young heir would marry the princess when the moment came.

Then the news came along the Silk Road that Kublai Khan had also died and the Polos finally felt free to head for home without further delay. After an emotional farewell to Koekoecin, they crossed Persia once more to Tabriz, where the Khan lived. They reached the Black Sea at Trebizond, boarded a ship bound for Constantinople, and from there headed back to Venice.

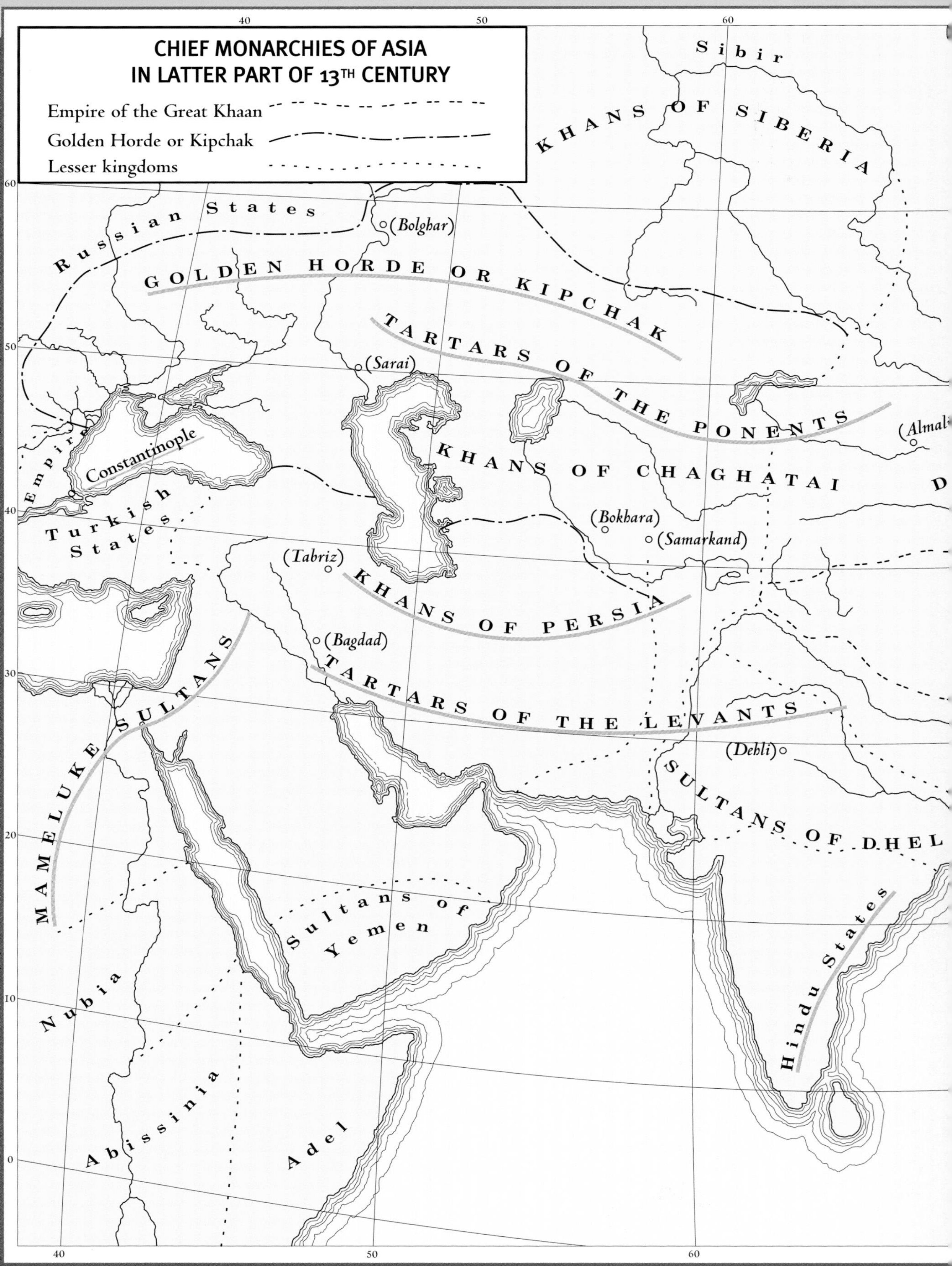
CHIEF MONARCHIES OF ASIA
IN LATTER PART OF 13TH CENTURY
Empire of the Great Khaan
Golden Horde or Kipchak
Lesser kingdoms
Sibir
KHANS OF SIBERIA
Russian States
(Bolghar)
GOLDEN HORDE OR KIPCHAK
TARTARS OF THE PONENTS
(Sarai)
Empire
Constantinople
KHANS OF CHAGHATAI
(Almali
Turkish States
(Bokhara)
(Samarkand)
(Tabriz)
KHANS OF PERSIA
(Bagdad)
TARTARS OF THE LEVANTS
MAMELUKE SULTANS
(Dehli)
SULTANS OF DHEL
Sultans of Yemen
Hindu States
Nubia
Abissinia
Adel
40
50
60
30
20
10
0

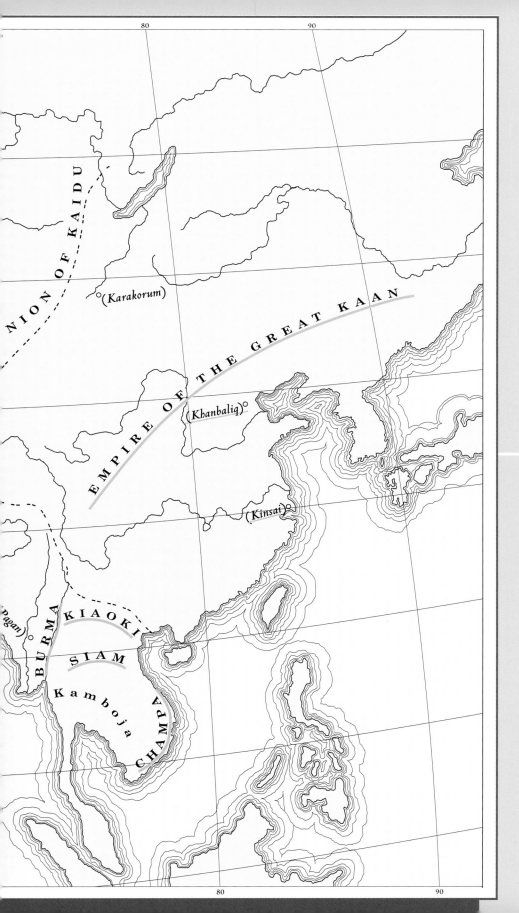

THE REALMS
OF ASIA

I N ADDITION TO YULE'S EXCELLENT WORK, THERE IS A MAP THAT ILLUSTRATES THE main Asiatic kingdoms during the thirteenth century. The huge expanse of the dominions belonging to Kublai Khan and the other Mongol rulers, which measured over 4,300 miles across, is immediately clear.

MICHAEL YAMASHITA

QUANZHOU, THE SOUTH CHINA SEA AND VIETNAM

IT WAS OUR LAST STOP IN CHINA, QUANZHOU, TO CONFIRM THE TRUTHFULNESS OF WHAT MARCO HAD WRITTEN.

Quanzhou was the largest port in the world when Marco lived in the country; today the city is no longer a port because over the last seven hundred years the estuary has silted up the bay and pushed the coast line farther downstream. It was here, in the mud, that archaeologists recently unearthed a spectacular find, a Chinese boat. In his book, as a fellow seafarer would, he described the Chinese style of boat in reverent terms. The Venetian said that the frame of Chinese boat was divided into thirteen "watertight compartments," exactly as seen in the excavated hull, and he added with admiration that the planking was formed by between two and six layers, a new layer being added every year. The boat found in Quanzhou had three and four layers of planks. This was the incontestable proof we had been looking for: without a doubt, Marco had been here. Marco also stated that the Quanzhou region has produced the best examples of Chinese porcelain. We checked the existence of a porcelain-making tradition here and quickly discovered that in Dehua – about 30 miles (or "five bridges" by Marco's estimation) northwest of the old port – the highest quality porcelain is still produced. We visited a crafts school and were surprised to find students working, not on traditional motifs, but on a bust of a Western boy of their same age.

From the vastness of inland Asia, Marco headed southward to even vaster waters of the South China Sea. Having worked extensively in Southeast Asia, I was familiar with these areas that Marco describes, including Vietnam. He is reputed to have touched down in Qhi Nhon, following the trade winds. He also writes about, though apparently without having visiting there, the thousands of islands that make up the Philippines. Marco likely never went farther east than China either, but his book makes reference to the Japanese archipelago, and he speaks of the shining gold roofs there, most likely referring to the Golden Pavilion in Kyoto. Kublai Khan was very interested in Japan, and had sent a large fleet to conquer that empire but the venture ended in disaster: the kamikaze, or the "divine wind" of a typhoon completely destroyed his forces just before they reached Japan. Almost nothing survived the typhoon, which saved the Japanese from Mongol domination. It was one of two times that typhoons were to destroy Kublai Khan's huge armada. Two centuries later, Marco's descriptions of Japan fascinated Christopher Columbus, who took a copy of his book with him to the Caribbean. After reading what Marco had to say about Japan, he was convinced that he had found Cipango, as the Italians called Japan, in the islands of the Caribbean. Discovering America was just a happy accident on his way to his real destination of Japan, lured on, like us, by the fabulous descriptions in Marco Polo's book.

ZAYTON
(QUANGZHOU)

Mekong River

VIETNAM
(CHAMBA)

DANANG

PHILIPPINES

Malaka Strait

South China Sea

SUMATRA

Pentain

○ City visited or described

○ Other major sites

••••••••• Homeward route

0   621 Miles

CERAMICS
SCHOOL

412-413 Pupils in the
ceramics school in Dehua –
where the best porcelain in
China is produced – copy the
bust of a Western boy.

414-415 Groups of fishing boats dot the placid waters of marvelous Halong Bay in the extreme north of Vietnam.

Da Nang
The new Vietnam

"You must know that on leaving the port of Zayton you sail west-south-west for 1500 miles, and then you come to a country called Chamba, a very rich region, having a king of its own."

The Travels of Marco Polo,
Vol. II, Bk. 3, Ch. 5

416-417 Da Nang, far from the new centers of power, is hectic and relatively wealthy.

Da Nang
The Heart of the Coast

418-419 A smiling fisherman in Da Nang
on the Vietnamese coast.

420-421 Squid are prepared for drying,
an indispensable process for conserving
the surplus catch.

Laboring in the saltworks
The sea fields

422 Emptying one pool after another, Vietnamese saltwork laborers finally get to the salt.

423 The crystalization of salt depends on regulating the water flow into the evaporation pools.

VIETNAM
FISHING ON STILTS

424-425 Tall bamboo stilts allow fishermen to follow fish into deeper waters.

426-427 Women separate the husk used for animal feed from the grain in a rice barn in Soc Trang, Vietnam.

THE MEKONG
DELTA
DOWN AMONG THE
MANGROVE SWAMPS

428-429 In the dawn haze, two
women go to market in Camau,
southern Vietnam.

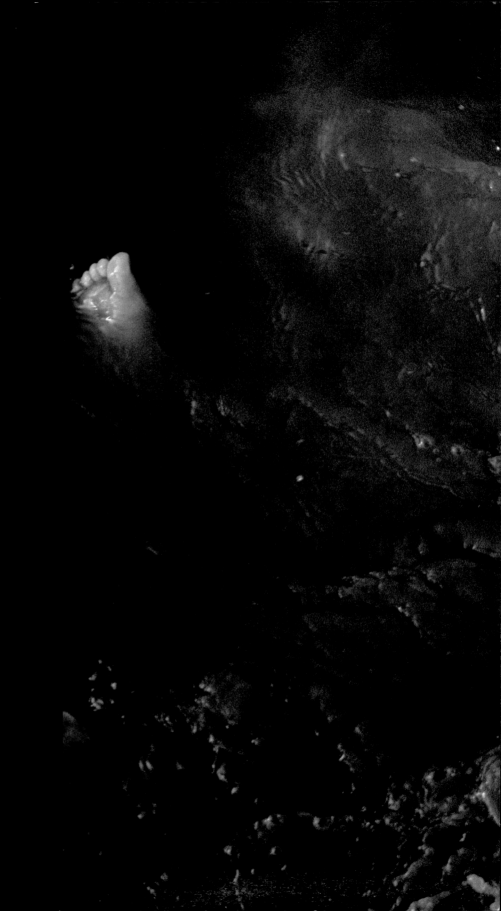

CAMBODIA
WATERGAMES IN PHNOM PENH

"Moreover, when you travel on that river, and come to a halt at night, unless you keep a good way from the bank the lions will spring on the boat and snatch one of the crew and make off with him and devour him."

The Travels of Marco Polo,
Vol. II, Bk. 2, Ch. 59.

430-431 Two children play in the mud-brown waters in Phnom Penh, where the Tonle Sap river joins the Mekong.

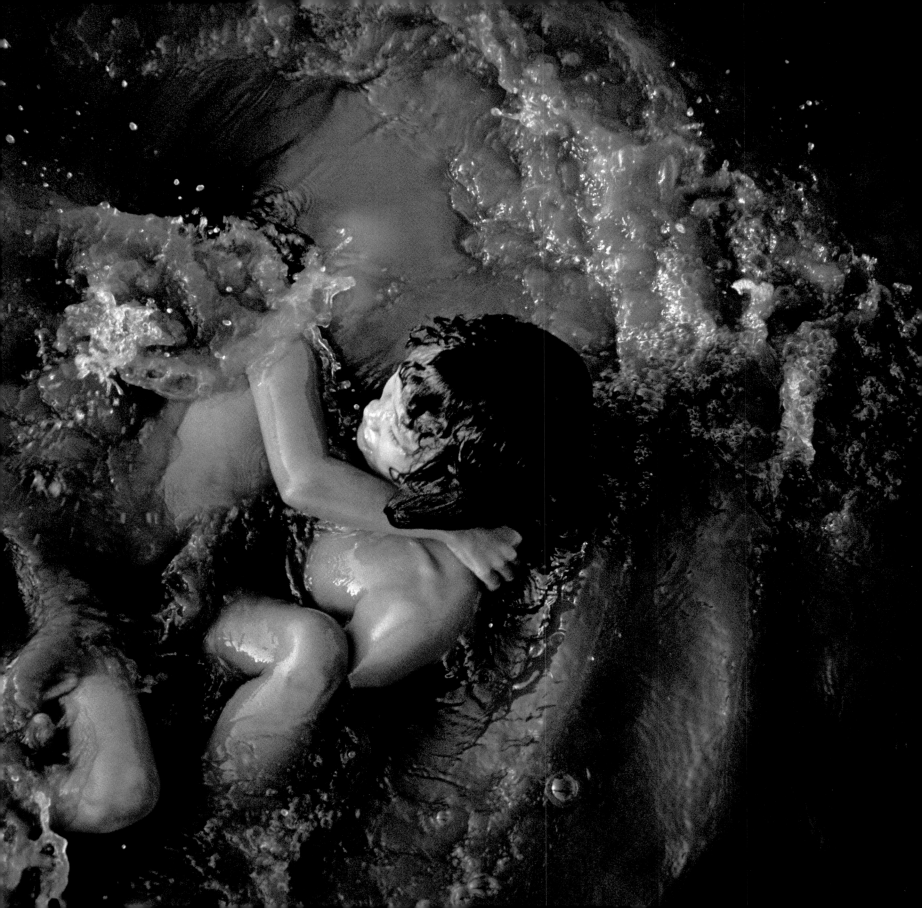

Tonle Sap
The unsalted sea

432-433 Fishermen strike the water with
sticks in the Tonle Sap basin in Cambodia,
hoping to frighten fish into their nets.

THE PHILIPPINES
A MYRIAD OF ISLANDS

434 The Philippine Archipelago comprises thousands of islands (7459 for Marco Polo) and lagoons, rich in timber, spices, wildlife and fish.

435 A Filipino fisherman surfaces with a large sea urchin.

FROM INDONESIA TO SRI LANKA

After coming this far with him, we couldn't very well leave Marco Polo in Asia.

We needed to see him home. It was the last challenge of our venture. Others had tried to follow Marco's journey from Venice to China and others had retraced his footsteps in China itself, but no one, as far as we know, had ever completed the entire round trip he described. When we presented the idea to our editors at the National Geographic, they answered, "Yes. Keep going. Bring him home. . . in two months."

We prepared for the long return that was to take us to places utterly different from those we had seen on the way out. From the bare, cold and dusty landscape of Central Asia, we were heading to the luxuriant, heavily populated islands in the perennially warm waters of the tropics.

After a journey south on the tail of the northeast monsoon, Marco got waylaid in the small kingdom of Samudra (now Sumatra, Indonesia) when the winds died down.

He was grounded here for five months, waiting for the summer southwest monsoon to give way to another southeast wind that would push him and his colleagues toward Persia via Sri Lanka and India.

Two things about Sumatra stood out to the homeward bound Venetian: the abundance of the fish in the waters that surround the large island and the presence of a people who, as he put it, "lived like beasts" and ate human flesh.

There's little evidence today of those things that made such a strong first impression on Marco. Pollution in the South China Sea has severely depleted marine wildlife, despite the fact that fishing is still an economic mainstay for Sumatrans.

When we reached the port of Belawan in the Strait of Malacca, the few fishing boats we saw were not in the harbor but were either being repaired or having the barnacles burned off their keels. It was hard to believe that Marco considered this the best fishing in the world.

Batak marriage

he bride and groom eat from a communal dish. The Batak pe

Great fishing wasn't the only reason Marco and his party hugged the coast during their five-month stay in Sumatra.

It was fear of a tribe of man-eating people, whom Marco didn't mention by name, but whom we know today as the Bataks, who live in the interior of the island.

Today, we were assured, they have found Christianity and long ago given up eating human flesh. We headed inland to the heart of the island where we were to attend a Batak wedding in Onan Raja, near Lake Toba. Here I photographed the tribe's striking "long houses," with exaggeratedly sloping roofs, and their residents in traditional costumes, most likely identical to the ones they wore when Marco was on Sumatra.

The groom was dressed in Western clothes and the bride in local costume, and they ate with their hands from a communal dish. I photographed a platter of fish whose contents looked vaguely like a human hand, at least to the more suggestible, and as we found out, the Bataks are good-humored about their gory past and often warn visitors "don't make us mad or. . . we'll eat you."

Marco also spoke of fantastic creatures like unicorns (in fact, rhinoceroes) and "men with tails. . .who live in the mountains and are a kind of wild men." Most likely he was talking about the timid and harmless orangutans, who now live in the protected forests of the island. It isn't hard to imagine that these animals are human, or at least have human characteristics, when one reaches out for your camera in curiosity and then strokes your hand with a motherly pat.

When the winds changed again, the Polos and their party were ready to leave Sumatra and its wild wonders to set sail for Sri Lanka.

Leaving the perils of Sumatra behind, Marco set sail for Sri Lanka (or Seilan, as he knew it), which he said was the most beautiful island of its size in the world.

Dominating the western province of Sri Lanka is Adam's Peak, a 7390-foot high summit that is sacred to three major religions: Buddhists believe the foot-shaped imprint in a rock on Adam's Peak is a sign of the Enlightened One; Muslims attribute it to Mohammed, and Christians believe it is the footprint of the first man.

We, like the many pilgrims who flock to the site, made our ascent on foot up the mountain. We climbed through the night so that we would arrive by dawn to shoot the spectacular view Marco wrote about. Though long, the climb went well until we made it to the summit. The only view we saw was clouds and mist.

Discouraged, I sat down and considered my options. After three hours, there was still no break in the clouds. Then suddenly, the sun appeared for five minutes, all I needed to make the frame I wanted.

A born merchant, Marco was fascinated by Sri Lanka's still renowned gem mines, known for their great variety of precious stones.

Miners still dig for stones in the mud from a rectangular trench, then rinse the sludge through a sieve. The stones are then cut and polished in Ratnapura, at the foot of Adam's Peak.

The morning we watched the process, miners extracted a handful of various stones from the mud — the most valuable being a large blue sapphire, worth about $2000.

Although Marco never wrote about tea, which was undoubtedly common in the thirteenth century, he devotes considerable attention to stronger drinks.

When discussing Sri Lanka, he mentions palm wine, which is still produced exactly as it was seven centuries ago.

Harvesting the palms for the wine is dangerous work: Gatherers climb up the curved slender trunks of the palms, and tap the trunk, as a Vermonter would do to draw sap from a maple. The palm juice flows from the taps and is caught in pots attached to the tree, then fermented to make a drink called toddy (*tari* in Hindi).

The harvesters, like tightrope walkers, move across cords that stretch between the trees over 100 feet from the ground, especially in the coastal area where we photographed them.

Beside toddy, Marco surely slaked his thirst with coconut milk, as he writes that there were "great quantities of Indian nuts, as big as a man's head, which are good to eat. The inside of the nut is filled with a liquor like clear fresh water, but better to the taste and more delicate than wine or any other drink that ever existed."

FROM INDONESIA TO SRI LANKA

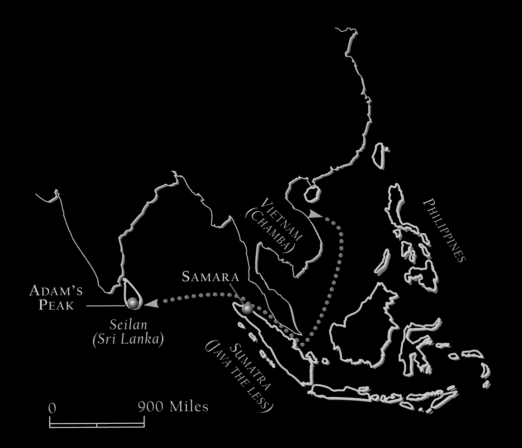

PHILIPPINES

VIETNAM
(CHAMBA)

SAMARA

ADAM'S
PEAK

Seilan
(Sri Lanka)

SUMATRA
(JAVA THE LESS)

● City visited or described

● Other major sites

•••••• Homeward route

0   900 Miles

BELAWAN
THE NETS OF MALACCA

"[...] you come to another kingdom called Samara, on the same Island. And in that kingdom Messer Marco Polo was detained five months by the weather, which would not allow his going on. [...] There is an abundance of fish to be had, the best in the world."

The Travels of Marco Polo,
Vol. II, Bk. 3, Ch. 10

442-443 Fishermen sort their nets in Belawan, a Sumatran port on the Strait of Malacca.

BELAWAN
WAR AGAINST BARNACLES

"When Messer Marco Polo was detained on this Island five months by contrary winds, [he landed with about 2000 men in his company; they dug large ditches on the landward side to encompass the party, resting on either end at the sea-haven, and within these ditches they made bulwarks or stockades of timber] for fear of these brutes of man-eaters [...]."

The Travels of Marco Polo,
Vol. II, Bk. 3, Ch. 10

444-445 – Barnacles damage fishing boat hulls; they must be removed with fire.

446 It is easy to understand how Marco Polo could describe orangutans as "men with tails [...] who live in the mountains."

447 Orangutans are shy and defenseless creatures; here one emerges from the forest in search of food and clean air.

ADAM'S PEAK
THE IMPRINT OF MAN'S FIRST FOOTSTEP

"[...] In the Island of Seilan there is an
exceeding high mountain; it rises right up so
steep and precipitous that no one could ascend
it, were it not that they have taken and fixed
to it several great and massive iron chains, so
disposed that by help of these men are able to
mount to the top. And [...] they say that on
this mountain is the sepulchre of Adam."

The Travels of Marco Polo,
Vol. II, Bk. 3, Ch. 15

448-449 Adam's Peak, in southern Sri Lanka,
emerges from the morning mists.

Tea Mountains

450-451 In certain areas of Sri Lanka,
altitude and humidity ensure the
growth of excellent tea bushes.

THE ISLAND OF GEMSTONES

452 Gems are mined in water-filled pits and shafts, often deep and with their sides buttressed by wooden nails

453 Precious stones are sieved and sorted before being sent to nearby Ratnapura for cutting and polishing.

INDIA

———◆———

FROM SRI LANKA, THE EXPEDI-
TION LED BY MARCO POLO HEADED
TOWARD INDIA. WE FOLLOWED HIM TO
KERALA, THE STATE ON THE SOUTHWEST
COAST OF THE SUBCONTINENT.

We arrived after dark in a fishing village, where a full moon illuminated a single thirty-foot double-ended rowboat that a dozen men were pushing into the water. The light on the long boat's graceful form was magical, but the fishermen advised me to return in the morning when there would be many more boats to photograph. The next day, we found the empty beach transformed into a throng of nearly naked people pulling in the nets that had been set the night before.

In a dance defined over the centuries, whole families worked together efficiently with perfect coordination and cooperation. Crashing through heavy surf, the boats rowed out beyond the breakers to close the nets and bring the lines to shore. The families on the shore would then rhythmically haul in the huge nets, now full of flopping fish, onto the beach. Each family member had a role to play; the men

pulled in and unloaded the heavy nets, the children helped pick out the fish caught in them, and the women went to work with knives, gutting and preparing the fish for market. In the whole operation, I never saw any tool or method any more modern than those that Marco might have witnessed in the thirteenth century.

We continued up the coast to Cochin, in search of more Marco Polo clues. We were rewarded with the sight of huge dip fishing nets, known to the Indians as "Chinese nets." I was familiar with this style of net from my work in China and Vietnam, but these were the largest dip-nets I had ever encountered. It's certain that Marco Polo would have come upon these huge nets, which are said to have been in use for centuries before his journey. Hundreds are still in use today.

The route Marco traveled, along the coast of India, is the route he first intended to take to China, but lack of suitable boats made the trip east along this Silk Route of the sea impossible. But on the way home, following trade winds, Marco had the chance to experience the mys-

HOLY MEN
SHIVA ASCETICS

456 In India - Chennai province - Cows have been worshiped in India for 3500 years.

460-461 While the sun dissolves the mist, fishermen of Kovalum, in Kerala, pull in their nets into the shallow water

teries of the ancient sub-continent as well as the hum of commerce that moved through the waters of the Indian Ocean. Though many merchant ships had traveled this route, Marco was the first to write about it. He witnessed the cross-cultural exchange that brought together an assortment of gem merchants, textile dealers, sea captains and spice traders from all over Asia.

To find and shoot the most valued of Indian spices, cardamon, we traveled inland. The women who harvest it labor in 100°F weather, dressed in colorful silk saris that look more like formal wear than work clothes, under a canopy of cardamon, the king of spices and the key aromatic ingredient of all Indian cuisine.

Many of India's traditions, including its cuisine, are largely based on religious beliefs and have evolved over three millennia, with few fundamental changes. While these traditions make India an amazing repository of the past, they sometimes collide with the rush of the modern world. The veneration of cattle is an example. The cows of India receive the highest respect of any bovines in the world, a fact which struck Marco as odd, but is a fact of Indian life. Cows are considered Hindu divinities, and are worshipped as such. People of every caste can be seen kissing cows in the temples as if they were sacred relics, which in a way

they are. Even in the chaotic streets of Indian cities, cows peacefully make their way undisturbed through traffic jams and pollution. Occasionally one might decide to lie down quietly in the middle of the street, where it stays as long as it likes, oblivious to the roar of the surrounding traffic. Someone might stop to feed it or place a garland of flowers around its neck, but otherwise the cow lies there undisturbed.

Cows are also prominently represented in temple statuary, along with all the other Hindu deities. A huge statue of the bull called Nandi, the mount of Siva, the most powerful and venerated god in the Hindu pantheon stands in Brihadiswara temple in Thanjavur (Tanjore), southwest of Madras. I photographed it as a priest standing on a scaffold poured a golden mixture of milk and curry over its head, an act of devotion that had been repeated for generations long before Marco might have seen it performed.

Marco, marveling that most Indians refused to eat beef, was also surprised by another custom linked to cow worship that still exists today in rural areas. That it has survived may be due as much to practicality as religious observance. The outside walls of houses are often smeared with cow dung, which is then decorated with intricate patterns drawn with a white powder, combining mysticism with utility, as the dung is actually an effective, if pungent, insect repellent.

Another tradition that stems from the past, both the ancient and the not so distant era of flower children and hippies, is that of the sadhu, long-haired ascetics who worship Siva. Proud and impressive, sadhus are seen seeking alms in most Hindu temples. Marco saw and described these holy men, whom he called "choghi," but he could not have known that he was actually describing the model for a flower child of the 1960s. When the Beatles went to India to study meditation from the Maharishi Yogi, they also learned the customs of the bearded sadhus who wore orange-colored clothing, strings of pearls and smoked marijuana for "spiritual enlightenment." The Beatles, along with other influential celebrities, introduced Indian mysticism and its trappings to Western audiences: peace, love, mind-expanding substances, brightly colored clothing, beads and long hair. But had they read his book, they would have known that Marco had seen it all, long before John Lennon ever sang about "instant karma."

Marco's description of the sadhus tells of "people that go naked ... because they do not want anything that is of this world." Sadhus still vow to renounce all worldly goods, and most wear only cotton wraps and never cut their hair, which can reach eight feet or more in length. But one holy man I met at a temple in Mumbai was shaved completely bald and had not worn a single item of clothing for almost fifty years, as if he had walked straight out of the pages of Marco's book.

The next stop on Marco's trail took us to the western tip of India, to the fertile but marshy plains of Gujarat from where he set sail on the last stretch of his journey towards the Persian Gulf to deliver his royal cargo. The main agricultural product of this region described by Marco is still cotton, India's most famous cotton. Said to have the most vivid colors in the world, it is spun, woven and dyed here. I've seen few more photogenic sights than the fields of Gujarat strewn end to end with washed and dyed cloth drying in the sun in kaleidoscopic patterns of brilliant color.

Gujarat was the springboard for the final stage of Marco's journey, which would send him back through Iran, Turkey and finally, home to Venice, where the great traveler had left when just a boy. He was returning 24 years later, bringing with him the most extraordinary collection of knowledge and experiences that a traveler has ever shared, not just with his countrymen, but to the world.

INDIA

Yamuna

DELHI ○

Ganges

Chambal

GUJARAT

BHAUNAGAR

TOWARD
HORMUZ ◄

MUMBAI

MALABAR

KERALA

○ City visited or described

● Other major sites

•••••• Homeward route

CHENNAI

COCHIN

0   360 Miles

Seilan
(Sri Lanka)

Kovalum
The past and the present

462 The young in the fishing villages of Kerala dress simply and suitably.

463 Traditional boats have no motor, just oars, each of which weighs about 50 pounds.

Kovalum
Life is the net

464 Last stages of net-cleaning. Nothing is wasted.

465 Fishing is a family affair: each family operates
its own boats and nets.

Kovalum

Fishing in the sand

"In all this Province of Maabar there is never a Tailor to cut a coat or stitch it, seeing that everybody goes naked! For decency only do they wear a scrap of cloth; and so 'tis with men and women, wih rich and poor, aye, and with the King himself."

The Travels of Marco Polo,
Vol. II, Bk. 3, Ch. 17

466-467 Daubed with silver scales, a young girl participates in the fish harvest.

468-469 Marco Polo's 'nuts of India': coconuts are shelled and dried in Kerala.

470-471 Hoping for a worthwhile catch, fishermen of Cochin, Kerala check their dip nets, a tradition imported from China.

472-473 Dusk on the Indian coast
of the Arabian Sea.

KERALA
NIGHT FISHERMEN

"[The pearl fishers] must also pay those
men who charm the great fishes, to prevent
them from injuring the divers [...]. These
fish-charmers are called Abraiaman; and
their charm holds good for that day only,
for at night they dissolve the charm so that
the fishes can work mischief at their will."

The Travels of Marco Polo,
Vol. II, Bk. 3, Ch. 16

474-475 Under a full moon, fishermen prepare
their boat for the night-time laying of the nets.

CHENNAI
RELIGION AND USEFULNESS

"And let me tell, you, the people of this country have the custom of rubbing their houses all over with cow dung."

The Travels of Marco Polo,
Vol. II, Bk. 3, Ch. 17

476-477 The cow dung decorations on this house in Chennai keep the insects away.

478-479 Deep and sincere veneration in Ganesh temple in Chennai.

TANJORE
CURRY FOR NANDI

"These people are Idolaters, and many of them worship the ox, because (say they) it is a creature of such excellence. They would not eat beef for anything in the world, nor would they on any account kill an ox."

The Travels of Marco Polo,
Vol. II, Bk. 3, Ch. 17

480-481 In Tanjore, a priest sprinkles the statue of the sacred bull Nandi with milk mixed with curry.

BRAHMIN WEDDING
THE FIRE THAT BONDS

482 A Brahmin celebrates a wedding in Chennai.

483 The priest throws rice grains onto the sacred fire,
in keeping with an ancient tradition.

484-485 In Mumbai, only the tiniest offering of incense is needed in the purification of a home.

"If anyone asks how it comes that they are not ashamed to go stark naked as they do, they say, 'We go naked because naked we came into this world, and we desire to have nothing [...]of this world. Moreover we have no sin of the flesh to be conscious of, and therefore we are not ashamed of our nakedness.'"

The Travels of Marco Polo,
Vol. II, Bk. 3, Ch. 20

MUMBAI
PARTING FROM THE MATERIAL WORLD

486 and 487 This 'naked sadhu' in Mumbai has
not worn clothes for fifty years.

THE ROUTE OF THE SADHU
ASCETICS IN ACTION

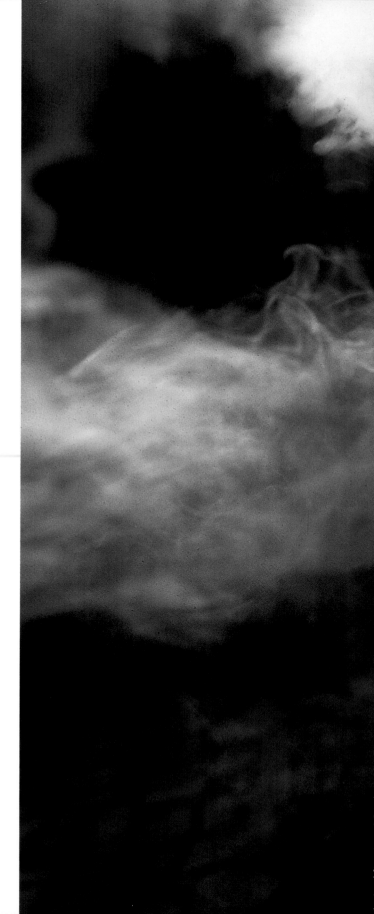

488 and 489 Sadhus in Mumbai achieve mystical states...
with the help of a great deal of marijuana.

Junagadh
Between ecstasy and
asceticism

"*There are certain members of this Order who
lead the most ascetic life in the world. [...]
Moreover they take cow-dung and burn it,
and make a powder thereof; and make an
ointment of it, and daub themselves withal.*"

The Travels of Marco Polo,
Vol. II, Bk. 3, Ch. 20

490-491 Sadhus gather regularly from all
over India. Here they are in Junagadh, in
Gujarat.

492

492-493 A dead holy man is carried to his funeral pyre in Junagadh.

494-495 Freshly-dyed cotton is laid out to dry in a field in Gujarat.

EPILOGUE

GENOA AND SEVILLE

The end of our story took us to where some say the Marco Polo story began – Korcula (Curzola) on the Dalmatian coast, now a part of Croatia.

Fittingly, I boarded the Marco Polo cruise ship for the overnight trip from Rijeken. Though it is Venice with whom Marco Polo is most associated, Korcula claims a piece of the Polo legend. The Korculans purport that he was born there, and it is Korcula that was the site of the sea battle between Venice and Genoa during which Marco was captured. Korcula, with its orange-roofed architecture reminiscent of Venice, even has a house facade and tower reputed to have once been the Polos. We even met Mr. Vladimir Depolo, a claimed descendant of Marco, whom I duly photographed in the Marco Polo tower overlooking the deep blue of the Adriatic.

But it is Genoa where the Marco Polo legend really began. Marco was imprisoned there by Venice's arch rivals at sea only three years after his return from China. It was pouring the day I arrived in Genoa; the weather seemed to be offering a comment on the indignity of locking up a man who had experienced the immensity of Asia and had served the master of the largest empire ever built. But of course, had there been no prison, there likely would have been no book and who knows how long the world would have had to wait to learn about the wonders he had seen.

Despite the rain, I was determined to photograph the building that had been Marco's jail, Palazzo San Giorgio, which still stands, though renovated over the centuries. However, the weather did not improve, so I decided to visit the Palazzo Doria Tursi, since I still needed a portrait of my traveling companion. There, high on a wall is a beautiful mosaic of a man with the clear and resolute gaze of an explorer, his face lit by the reflection of gold tiles and framed by a large flowing beard. He looks to the right, toward the East, though perhaps this is just coincidence. In this portrait Marco seems about forty, roughly his age when he returned to Venice.

When I left the Palazzo Doria, it was still raining so I decided to wait out the storm, as

Marco Polo expression

The Traveller's look

In this mosaic kept in Pal   Doria Tursi in Genoa, Marco Polo seems read

zzo SAN
ORGIO
LLER IN CHAINS

azzo San Giorgio, in
arco Polo's prison after
t the battle of Curzola

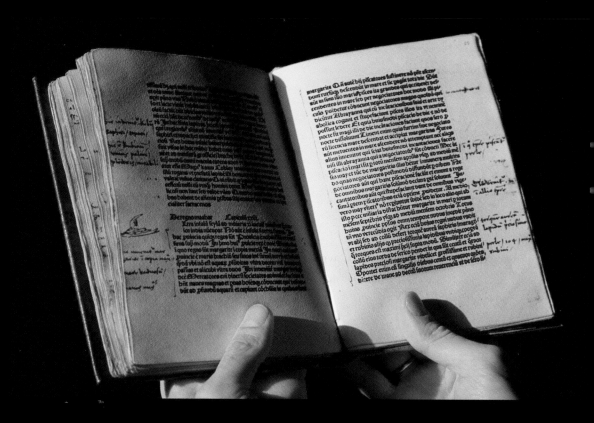

COLUMBUS'S DREAM
IDEAS FOR NEW DISCOVERIES

500 Christopher Columbus was a careful reader of *Il Milione*: he filled his copy of the book (now in Seville) with margin notes.

Marco might have, by eating a plate of pasta near the port. After a while the sun broke out from behind the clouds and, within minutes, the day turned radiant. I returned to the old prison, and as I was considering how to get the best angle on the building, I looked down and saw its elaborate façade perfectly reflected in a large puddle. This let me "suspend" the building in a dimension outside of time, just as I had tried to do throughout the trip. As I was about to shoot a frame, the reflected profile of a bird in flight appeared — the final element I needed. The shadow of the bird stood out almost surreally against the building and provided a sense of freedom and space, a symbol of the unstoppable desire to soar beyond one's limits.

As a fitting postscript to our adventure with Marco, we traveled to Spain, where Marco's book had helped to convince another great explorer of the possibility of reaching China without crossing the entire continent of Asia, and without falling off the earth. We wanted to photograph Christopher Columbus's own Latin copy of The Description of the World, the one he took with him on his voyage of discovery in 1492. We found it at the Columbus Library in Seville. It is clear that the sailor had read it carefully, scrupulously making notes, and even doodles, on the pages that seemed to him most important.

Perhaps Columbus was more idealistic or impulsive than Marco, but he would certainly have appreciated the uniqueness that distinguished Marco's recounting from similar works of the period. Traditional travel writing in Marco's day was guided by superstitious religiosity and imbued with extravagant imagination. The world found in most travel accounts of the Middle Ages was populated by men with two heads and feet that faced backwards, by animals that were wilder than in the most hair-raising medieval bestiary, by lands that burned eternally, and by seas of blood or wine. There was little concrete, verifiable information. Marco's book is the opposite: Despite doubts raised by some scholars, there is nothing that comes close to it in terms of accuracy, variety and detail. Marco was a pioneer, in exploration, but more importantly of a groundbreaking modern outlook, that combined curiosity and courage with humanity and intelligence.

That is why we, as fellow travelers, wanted to pay tribute, in the face of modern skepticism, to the account of a great man who lived seven hundred years ago and who, despite the centuries that separate us, was able to lead us like a close friend along the paths of his — and our — world.

BIOGRAPHIES

MICHAEL YAMASHITA has for over two decades combined his twin passions – photography and travel – as a regular contributor to National Geographic, working in such diverse locations as Somalia and Sudan, Great Britain and Ireland, New Guinea and New Jersey. He has traveled to the six continents, but Asia is his area of primary concentration. He has lived in Singapore, Thailand, Hong Kong and Japan, and has taken photographs for a variety of Asian publications. Yamashita has authored five books including: *The Mekong: A Journey on the Mother of Waters* (Takarajima Books), – tracing the Mekong from its sacred source in China down to the South China Sea and *In the Japanese Garden* (Starwood) written by his wife Elizabeth Bibb, which received the American Booksellers Association Benjamin Franklin award. In addition to his own books Yamashita has participated in five *A Day in the Life of... books*. He is a member of a select group of photographers whose work is included in six Asian book projects published by Paris-based Didier-Millet: *China: The Long March*; *Malaysia*; *Indonesia*; *Brunei*; and *The Philippines* and *Vietnam*. Mike Yamashita has received numerous professional awards, including the National Press Photographers Association (NPPA) Pictures of the Year Competition, New York Art Director's Club; Asian-American Journalists Association (AAJA); and the Pacific Area Travel Association (PATA). His work has been displayed at the National Gallery of Art (United States), the Los Angeles County Museum of Art, and Kodak's Professional Photographer's Showcase at Epcot Center, Orlando, Florida. When not on assignment Yamashita is at home in New Jersey where he is a volunteer fireman. **Please visit www.michaelyamashita.com.**

GIANNI GUADALUPI, has worked for thirty years as a writer, translator, and anthology editor, dealing in particular with nonfictional and fictional travel writing. He is co-editor of *Le Vie del Mondo*, a magazine published by the Italian Touring Club. He edits the *Guide Impossibili* (Impossible Guides), *Antichi Stati* (Ancient States), and *Grand Tour* collections for Franco Maria Ricci. Among his works on the culture of travel are: *China as Seen by the Jesuits* (1980), Qajar: Voyages and Adventures in Nineteenth-Century Persia (1982), *A Dictionary of Fantastic Places* (1982), *Dictionary of the Interplanetary Traveler* (1983), *Voyages, Adventures, and Conquests of the Portuguese in the Indies* (1984), *Orients: Travel Writers of the Nineteenth Century* (1989), *The Newly Discovered America* (1991), *The Rajahs' Land: Passages to India from the Seventeenth to the Eighteenth Century* (1993), and *The World's Skies: Italian Aeronautical Adventures* (1994). He is the author of *The Discovery of the Nile* (White Star, 1997) and he edited *The World's Greatest Treasures* (White Star, 1998), and wrote the historical section of *The Art of Being a Lion* (White Star, 2002).

BIBLIOGRAPHY

Hart, Henry H., Marco Polo, Venetian Adventurer, University of Oklahoma Press, 1967.

Larner, John, Marco Polo and the Discovery of the World, Yale University Press, 1999

Moule, A. C. and Pelliot, P., The Description of the World, Routledge, London, 1938.

National Geographic Magazine, May, June, July 2001 issues, Washington, D.C.

Olschi, Leonardo, Marco Polo's Asia, Cambridge University Press, 1960.

Waldron, Arthur, The Great Wall of China: From History to Myth, Cambridge University Press, 1990.

Wood, Frances, Did Marco Polo Go to China? Secker and Warburg, London, 1995.

Yule, Sir Henry (ed.), The Travels of Marco Polo, London, 1870; Dover Publications, NY, 1993 (paperback).

PHOTO CREDITS

All photographs are by Michael Yamashita except the following:

Page 1: Giovanni Dagli Orti; page 7: Nader Davoodi; page 66: Marisa Montibeller; page 19 right: Antonio Attini/Archivio White Star; pages 19 left, 26 bottom, 36-37, 52-53, 216-217: Archivio White Star; pages 21, 24, 26 top, 28, 29, 31, 32-33, 34, 35, 44, 45, 47, 48, 49, 50, 51, 209, 210, 212, 214, 215, 400, 401, 402, 403, 404, 406, 407: Bibliothèque Nationale de France, Paris; pages 22, 23: Double's; pages 25 top, 27, 30, 43, 211: Photos 12; page 213: Bodleian Library, University of Oxford; pages 38-39: WorldSat International. The Publisher would like to thank Ms Maude Bernaud and the entire staff at the Bibliotèque Nationale de France for the solicit collaboration offered.

ACKNOWLEDGEMENTS

I WOULD LIKE TO THANK, first and foremost, my editors at National Geographic Magazine for making this book possible. From the proposal stage to final publication of an 80-page, three-part series in May, June and July 2001, the Marco Polo project took four years to complete. No other magazine in the world goes to such lengths to bring compelling stories to their readers. Thanks to Bill Allen, Editor in Chief, for first giving me the green light; to former editors Bob Poole and Al Royce, for their enthusiasm for the project; to Director of Photography Kent Kobersteen and Assistant Director Susan Smith for keeping me in film and finances for the two years it took to complete the shooting. Thanks also to Connie Phelps, head of layout, for her artful design of the story and to writer Tom O'Neill, for the great photo captions. Special thanks to Susan Welchman, my picture editor, for picking the best frames and offering guidance in the field. And thanks to my colleague and comrade in travel, Senior Staff Writer Mike Edwards, who was always there in the toughest countries and situations with a warm smile and encouraging words. Thanks for sharing the adventure and capturing it so eloquently.

Thanks also to my publisher and old friend Marcello Bertinetti of White Star (whom I first met on a train in Italy 20 years ago) and to Valeria Manferto De Fabianis, his partner and co-founder of White Star. I've enjoyed working with their excellent staff, especially Maria Valeria Urbani Grecchi, Clara Zanotti and Enrico Lavagno for putting my thoughts into Italian. Thanks to my assistants, interpreters, guides and consultants on the road: in Italy, to Carlo Roberti and Erla Zwingle, with special thanks to photographer Marisa Montibeller; in Iran to Nader Davoodi, Souryeh Kabiri and driver Farhad; in Iraq to Mohammed Fatnan and driver Samil Ahmad Mahmud; in Tajikistan to John Barbee and Joe McIntyre of UNOSHA. who got our gear out of Afghanistan; in Afghanistan to Haji Rashudin, Abdul Wahid, driver Agha and Boz Mohamed of the UN for getting us safely out of the country; in China to Ding Mingtang, Gao Jian, Zhu Yu (Ruby) and Anwar Jan Umar; in Hong Kong to How Man Wong and Alan and Han Yamashita; and in Myanmar to Brett and Omar Melzer and Myo Myo Myint of Balloons Over Bagan—thanks for the fantastic flight!

I thank Robert Kirschenbaum of Pacific Press Service in Japan, Tantyo Bangun in Indonesia and Dominic Sansoni in Sri Lanka, and in India Asif Khan and Neha and Vinay Diddee. Thanks also to friends at home: Bill Marr for his expert design sense; Alexandra Avakian for her help and contacts in Iran; Steve McCurry for his advice on India and Afghanistan; Tony Shugaar and Lisa Lytton for their publishing expertise; to Ira Block for his comforting calls to my cell phone in every part of the world; to Julie Qualmann, my studio manager, who holds down the fort while I'm away, and to Suzanne Goldstein of PPS for her good counsel.

Thanks to my wife, Elizabeth Bibb, who edits my manuscripts, takes loving care of our daughter Maggie, and keeps the home fires burning.

And finally, special thanks to my close friend Ann Judge. After sending me safely around the world for more than 20 years as head of the National Geographic Travel Department, Ann was killed on the flight that tore into the Pentagon on September 11, 2001. We miss you a lot, Ann.